THE OTHER REVOLUTION

russian

evangelical

awakenings

Geoffrey H. Ellis
and
L. Wesley Jones

A·C·U
PRESS

The Other Revolution

A·C·U PRESS

ACU Station, Box 29138
Abilene, TX   79699

Type Specifications: Headline set in DemocraticaRegular, 36 point, normal width. Body copy set in Palatino, 12 point. Endnote set in Palatino, 10 point.

Typesetting and page design by Ladybug Publishing.
Cover design by Robert Boman.

Printed in the United States of America

ISBN 0-89112-022-X

Library of Congress Card Number 96-085782

1,2,3,4,5

Wives who serve, pray and encourage are so special. Therefore, to Doreen Ellis and Beverly Jones we affectionately dedicate these pages.

In days remembered or known through the memories of
    others
that heavy white blanket of snow known as Russian Winter
has buried more than the fallen leaves of Golden Autumn
more than the harvested fields of the Ukraine
more than the summer sins of St. Petersburg
and that chilling cold called Russian Winter
has killed more than the weak robin unable to migrate
more than the green twig whose sap ran too long
more than the chrysanthemums who boldly bloomed
until they froze.

This poet soul grieves.

"This year, this Russian Winter ahead,
What will die from the chilling cold?
What will be buried under the heavy white blanket?"
From without the Tricolor came proud and the Swastika
came hard
but the chilling cold killed them
and the heavy white blanket buried them
and the enemy was gone and the enemy was broken.
From within grew unrest and anger
and the tsars fell to the chilling cold
and the hope of freedom mistakenly buried with them
under the heavy white blanket
and a new enemy had emerged, stronger than the old.

"Would St. Petersburg survive until spring
or would Leningrad
once more again be born in the snow?"

The Russian Winter would tell, but not yet.

—Charles K. Lehnbeuter, November 1993

contents

introduction

Russians' hunger for Bibles appeared as a national phenomenon when Soviet communism, cracked open by *glasnost*, gave way to republican movements. This is indeed a curiosity since Russian Orthodox Christianity, with a proud, thousand-year heritage, is not rooted in a Bible-focused tradition. The explanation for this enthusiasm, in large measure, may be found in the evangelical awakening which swept Russia during the last quarter of the nineteenth century and the first quarter of this century. So effective was this back-to-the-Bible movement that seventy years of repression by state-sponsored atheism served only to sharpen the hunger pangs for God's holy book.

The trail we followed as authors in investigating the Russian awakening led to an adventure of discovery. Our early lack of knowledge about the details and scope of the movement reflect the widespread lack of awareness, both in the West and the East. Such "general amnesia" is understandable: the awakening was vigorously suppressed by the Russian imperial government prior to 1917. Furthermore, the Stalinists determined to stamp out all vestiges of religion. Two "hot" wars and the subsequent "cold" war effectively blocked the churches of the West from either understanding or collaborating with Russian believers. Current secular histories seem little interested in pursuing the religious dimension. Blocked from public retelling, the story faded, with just the echoes—a lingering spiritual hunger and a passion for the Word of God—remaining as evidences of the earlier vibrant

Russian evangelicalism.

We soon found that a considerable archival record of the movement exists in Russia. Also, several instructive Western studies came subsequently to hand. Greater openness in Russia has encouraged a re-examination of their roots by Orthodox and denominational groups. What is missing, however, is a reflection on that bold period of revival near the turn of the century that assesses the Bible's penetration of Russian society as a powerful redirecting force, identifies the uniquely Russian attributes of this indigenous, Bible-only movement, and affirms the parallel between that time and ours. This book is prepared as a encouragement to learn from the past in order to be cheered for the future. The answer, both then and now, for Russia's spiritual and social plight comes not from the East, nor from the West, but from above. That answer is contained in the good news revealed in Jesus Christ through the inspired pages of the Word of God, increasingly available once again to the Russian people.

In 1989, Edward Bailey, vice-president of World Christian Broadcasting Corporation, came into the office of Wesley Jones, follow-up director for WCBC, with a few pages about the work of V. A. Pashkov, a nineteenth-century religious reformer, and asked if the information was familiar. It was not, but was immediately intriguing. Wesley, recipient of thousands of letters in response to short-wave broadcasting into Russia, had already been struck by a frequent identification by the correspondents: "I am a gospel Christian."[1] Could there be a connection? Despite our early belief that we were searching for a needle in a haystack, considerable information was soon located in the archives of the Disciples of Christ Historical Society in Nashville, Tennessee.

For several years prior to and following the 1917

Revolution, the American Disciples had been in touch
with the Russian evangelical movement. Were they
accurate in their enthusiastic assessment of the Russian
development as a "restoration movement" comparable
to their own tradition? What was the movement's scope,
its significance in Russia? Was there a Russian
recollection of this portion of history? Does this earlier
experience have any relevance for Russia in its present
plight? The answers to these and other questions could
only be found in Russia itself. Wesley reached out to
two friends: Tim Tucker, a professor of history who
resides in Finland, and Geoffrey Ellis, Canadian
evangelist and student of restoration history.
Preparations were made to enter Russia in August 1991.
With Dr. Tucker curtailed from further trips due to
health, Jones and Ellis returned in 1992, 1993 and 1995
for further investigations.

This work, couched in the contemporary
condition, is chiefly concerned with telling the story of
the Russian evangelical awakening during the years
1874-1928. It details the development as a direct
consequence of the availability of the Scriptures in the
Russian vernacular precisely at the time when
widespread acceptance was possible—the years of social
reform following the freeing of the serfs in 1861 under
Tsar Alexander II. This examination concludes that for
a brief time the revival was a viable alternative to the
nihilistic developments which led ultimately to the
revolutionary overthrow of the imperial regime. It
chronicles a growth—despite unrelenting opposition—
which was sufficient to change forever the heart of
Russia. The work is submitted with the belief that the
Russian spiritual soil has been cultivated by decades of
hardship and struggle. We believe that the planting of
the seed by the "gospel Christians" movement will
finally result in an unparalleled harvest in Russia during
the third millennium.

Primary sources located in Russia will be detailed in the following pages. Secondary works that proved especially valuable include Patricia Kennedy Grimsted, *Archives and Manuscript Repositories in the USSR, Moscow and Leningrad, 1976*; Edmund Heier, *Religious Schism in the Russian Aristocracy, 1860-1900: Radstockism and Pashkovism*, 1970; Hans Brandenburg, *The Meek and the Mighty: The Emergence of the Evangelical Movement in Russia*, 1977. Made available to the authors through unusual circumstances was *History of the Evangelical Christian-Baptists of the USSR*, 1989[2]. Ivan Prokhanov's 1933 autobiography *In the Cauldron of Russia, 1869-1933*, published in a new edition in 1993 by One Body Ministries of Joplin, Missouri, was also most useful.

The research would not have been possible by the unilingual authors were it not for the excellent work of Ludmila Baronova, Lydia Loginova and Yuri Dobrokhotov, each excellent as guide/interpreter/translator. The authors are indebted to the counsel of Thom Lemmons, managing director of A.C.U. Press, and to Carolyn Thompson for her indefatigable efforts as copy editor. We are grateful as well for the reading of the manuscript and helpful suggestions of Andrei Orlov and Dr. Tim Tucker.

We are well aware of the barriers posed by language and culture and of personal limitations in historical perspectives. The reader is invited to reach beyond any weaknesses or errors detected to the essential hopefulness of the work—the blessings that God has in store for his people in Russia.

---

[1] For an exciting glimpse into the mind of present-day Russians revealed in this correspondence, see L. Wesley Jones, *The Real Russians* (Huntsville, AL: Publishing Designs, Inc., 1995).

[2] Written in Russian, with excerpts translated by Lydia Loginova.

PART ONE

I

The Journey

Our Aeroflot flight on the tired Illushyn jet touched down at the Sheremetyevo airport in Moscow at 7:30 in the morning on that fateful Monday. The date was August 19, 1991.

The first words spoken by Sasha, who had driven out from the city to greet us, were, "Gorbachev has been arrested!" Clearly agitated, he had just received this disturbing news over his car radio on the way to the airport. Upon relaying the news the station, a new, private broadcaster, fell ominously silent.

Struggling to grasp the implications, we blurted, "Then, who's in charge?" "The fascists!" came the reply. The Russian Coup had begun, "The Third Russian Revolution" as it was called by *Newsweek*.

Thus began our week in Moscow. We had dedicated these days to researching an evangelical movement in Russia's capital city. Instead, the events of the three-day coup held the world's uneasy attention. Our personal agenda was effectively obliterated.

Tanks and military vehicles were strung along the roads as we made our way into the city. Sasha was clearly anxious to deliver his passengers, not least because his wife and child were vacationing in the country. Thoughts for them and worries about an imminent, armed confrontation were his uppermost concerns.

Our immediate destination was Chuck Whittle's apartment on Mechanistiya Lane, near the Moscow Olympic facilities. Upon our arrival we placed a call to Alexei, who was to be our translator and guide. Alexei, who works late and rises late, had not yet heard the news. Greatly disturbed, he said, "I must hang up now. I will get back to you!" He never did. Clearly, our plans for the week in Moscow were on hold, at the very least. After Moscow, our original itinerary called for investigations in Irkutsk, Siberia and Donetsk, Ukraine—two remote areas best to be avoided if civil war engulfed the country! Other calls were made to contacts in the city. One sought to calm us. "Don't worry. This is not about you. This is a deep habit with us!"

A remarkable and encouraging week had just been concluded in Leningrad. We had come to Moscow on the trail of the "Gospel Christians." Our search was for evidence of any lingering Russian consciousness of the evangelical awakening of a century earlier. This development had paralleled the socialist revolution leading up to 1917. The story was known in some detail in the West. It appeared to us that a significant spiritual advance had been made at a critical stage in Russian history. Further, we believed that the answers found earlier by Russian people had a powerful relevance for the troubled times currently faced by Russia. The conditions present at the collapse of the Tsarist Empire and those at the collapse of the Soviet Empire were similar, we felt. These powerful transitional periods were each preceded by great turmoil and followed by times of both despair and hopefulness. Perhaps the lessons of the past could give direction to Russia as it entered the Third Millennium.

For the next three days, we were eyewitnesses to the events which would change the face of the world. We saw the barricades go up on Kalinin Street and read the decrees posted by the coup leaders. We witnessed the tanks assembling and the intervening human barrier massing around the "White House," the seat of the Russian parliament, where Yeltsin, the defiant president of Russia, took his stand. We watched the people parading in the streets with voices sounding a newly found resolve and with faces resolute for a new day. We sensed the tension as the hours passed. Would the shooting begin? Would Russia be convulsed in another decimating civil war?

We spent much of Tuesday at the commercial office of the American embassy in a vain attempt to secure a fax line to North America. On Wednesday, with the help of Petr, an aspiring young Russian preacher for the Evangelical Christian-Baptist Church, we made preparations to return to Leningrad. Both American and Canadian embassies had advised Westerners to leave the country. We returned to our apartment by four in the afternoon. Ten minutes later the phone rang. Sasha, ever the bearer of dramatic news, announced, "The coup has failed!" With arrangements set, days lost, and uncertainty still in the air, we decided to proceed on our trip home.

Thursday morning, during a four-hour delay for the departure to Leningrad, we joined the crowds in the terminal lounge and witnessed the televised return of Gorbachev to Moscow. Later, before the TV screen in a hotel lobby in Leningrad, we experienced the rapt attention of a large gathering as it heard the restored leader of the Russian Republic give his speech. Gorbachev had endured the arrest by the hard-liners, but he would not survive the collapse of his world, so dramatically altered by the past three days.

It was to become clear that the Soviet system had been bankrupt for some time. The exiled writer Solzhensitsyn, as early as 1979, had protested, "Yes, we are still the prisoners of communism, and yet for us in

Russia, communism is a dead dog, while for many people in the West it is still a living lion."[1] As one well-educated Russian observed, "Our system produced the best scientists and engineers in the world. But we had no way to bring the benefits of their work to the people, or to bring the real strengths of the people to their work." The people were determined that yesterday's tyranny would be replaced by tomorrow's transformation. The failed coup came to symbolize the collapse of a hated regime. It signaled the opening to a new day for a modern Russia. New frontiers, new opportunities, a new spirit, and new leaders—those who could capture fresh visions—were becoming available. Russia would be a leader in the world again, but only after its soul was restored. Our journey to Russia in search of the turn-of-the-century awakening had taken on a dramatic relevance.

During our few hours with Petr as he assisted us in securing a flight back to Leningrad, we shared together our faith, our dreams and visions for the future. Finally, we asked him, "Are you familiar with Pashkov and Prokanov?" Petr's face broke into a broad smile. "Oh, yes," he said, "they are our leaders!" Then he proceeded to supply a serendipity. "I have a book in my library which tells their story, and I want you to have it." We made our way to the apartment which he shared with his mother, occupied by his family since before the days of the 1917 Revolution. From Petr's library of ten thousand volumes, of which he was justifiably proud, he selected the volume and presented it to us. Published in 1989, it contained a history of the very "Gospel Christians" whom we had come to research![2] Yes, it was apparent that a Russian awareness of Russia's spiritual past existed.

If the second week of our 1991 Russian trip was filled with excitement and significance, our earlier week, spent in Leningrad (shortly to return to its original name, "St. Petersburg"), was no less rewarding in discovery and symbolism. Our first stop was at the Saltykov-Shchedrin State Public Library. This library, with its twenty-five million items, had received the Order of Lenin. In its expansive reading room, Lenin had spent many hours perfecting the discipline from which he would exhort his followers to "study, study, study!" His portrait and plaque, hanging at the entrance to the reading room, seemed to offer an excellent opportunity for our photo record. When the light flashed, great consternation was expressed by the librarians attending us, along with embarrassment by our translator-guide, Ludmila Baronova. "You could be ejected! You could lose your camera!" Chastened, we nevertheless retained the photo as a valued reminder of those early moments in Saltykov-Shchedrin.

At first, the librarians were distant and cool. No, it was not likely that there would be any material of the kind we sought. Had we, in fact, been misguided or unjustified in thinking that such events as those introduced to us by a few North Americans were significant to any Russians? Could this thing have been "done in a corner," to use Paul's phrase? Had someone made a mountain of a mole-hill? These thoughts ran through our minds as we heard the first negative responses. However, with Ludmila's patient skill, the workers warmed to our quest. Index trays were produced, since no computer data-bases were yet available in this library. However, we found that any selected item could be produced within ten minutes of our request. Soon, an index card was found for the book *Gusli*, identifying Ivan Prokhanov as author and published in 1902. This Russian word was not familiar to our searchers. A dictionary was consulted. The "gusli" was a stringed instrument, sometimes used when hymns were sung. We had located a hymnbook. Published hymnals indicated a community of worshippers. We were on the right trail! Soon Ludmila was reading one reference after another to significant literature, persons and events of the Christians-only movement we had come to study! We were learning to say, "*Slava Bogu*"—Praise God!

Soon, evidence was uncovered of an extensive collection of writings from Prokhanov, an outstanding leader of the "Evangelical Christians" in the early decades of the twentieth century. There surfaced multiple versions of hymnbooks as well as all the issues of a Russian church paper, *The Christian*, begun in 1906 and continued until 1914 without interruption, then again sporadically from 1924 until 1928. We found miscellaneous books and papers and a fortnightly news magazine, *Morning Star*, published from 1910 until 1914. Clearly, the presence of the Gospel Christians was noted in their day and their memory was deemed worthy of preservation in the central archives of Leningrad.

When we finally took our leave of the librarians, it seemed that they were as excited as we, having given solid assistance in reaching our goals. Later that fall we unexpectedly received from Lydia, one of the librarians who assisted us in Saltykov-Shchedrin, an extended list of references to works detailing the Prokhanov/ Evangelical Christian movement. The following year we would return to examine these sources firsthand and to secure photocopies of selected portions of the material.

On Wednesday of that first week, we intended to visit the Museum of Religion and Atheism. The museum displays were housed in the impressive Kazan Cathedral, situated on Nevsky Prospekt and built in 1811 in the style of St. Peter's in Rome. Included in the exhibits, we had heard, were instruments of torture purported to have been used by the Church to keep its people "faithful." Disappointment came, however, as we learned that the museum was closed on Wednesdays. Not deterred, Ludmila led us to another church nearby. We picked our way through construction debris to a small office at the rear of the edifice. There, her negotiating skills much in evidence, Ludmila wrangled permission for a special viewing.

Dazzled by the splendor of the interior of the Kazan, we were immediately guided by an attendant away from the main collection to a special exhibit. On display was the record of Russia's sectarian movements! Twenty groups were included, and the Evangelical Christians were listed in the second position, following the Baptists.

Ample space was given for the presentation of photographs and text. There was a picture of Prokhanov taken in Chicago in 1912. There was a poster announcing a choral presentation by a choir of the Evangelical Christians, scheduled for March 29, 1989, in the Kazan Cathedral itself. Paydirt! Could we take pictures? No, pictures were not permitted, as the museum was closed on Wednesday! Come back tomorrow at 10:00 a.m., but be sure to be on time, since the exhibit was to be dismantled during the day.

We returned promptly at 10:00 next morning. Work in removing the special exhibit had already begun. We were directed, however, through a small door, up five flights of a narrow staircase into a magnificent medieval-style library. Before us was the 180-year-old cathedral collection!

Soon, index trays were again placed before us. Whereas the Saltykov-Shchedrin sources featured Prokhanov and the twentieth-century movement, the Kazan material proved to be a major trove regarding Vasili Pashkov and the Gospel Christians of the nineteenth century. These were works that presented

Orthodoxy's opposition to the "sectarians." The number of items in this collection confirmed the importance given by the Russian Orthodox Church to the threat posed by the evangelical movement. For example, there was a church paper which included an exchange between Colonel Vasili Pashkov and the chief priest of St. Isaac's cathedral. Pashkov explained why he was leaving the Orthodox Church, and the priest explained why he should not! We secured permission to remove several works from the library for photocopying. On our departure, we were presented with the Sostradane choral poster which had been a part of the special exhibition. We left the Kazan elated and astonished.

Only later did we realize the full significance of those two days at the Kazan. The final days of the "Russian Sectarian Movements" exhibition coincided with our schedule. Because of the events of the following week, the Museum of Religion and Atheism was, to all intents and purposes, finished, along with Russian Communism as the world knew it. In effect, we witnessed the closing of an institution, symbolic of the defeat of the seventy-year effort to enthrone atheism as the state religion of Russia!

Sunday afternoon, August 18, found us in an apartment on the outskirts of Leningrad. We were gathered with a dozen believers for the purpose of worship and fellowship. Included was Milana, a university student who had translated for us on the previous Wednesday and Thursday evenings at the Academy of the Arts, where the gospel was preached. Regular listeners of World Christian Broadcasting had filled the auditorium. Following the two evenings of teaching and the exchange of questions and answers, three indicated a desire to be baptized. Yuri, Lydia, and Tamara were baptized in Lake Ozerski the next day. These were with us at the Sunday gathering, along with two university students who were baptized that Sunday in Volodya's bathtub. Coincidentally, their names were Slava (meaning "Praise") and Vim (named by his father from the Russian acronym VMR—*Velikaya Mirya Revolutisia*—"Great World Revolution").

During the fellowship meal, the new Christians shared their joy over their baptism into Christ. They turned to the several present who had yet to make a commitment and asked if they would like to be baptized. Viktor, who had attended the meetings of the week before, agreed that he would but perhaps would wait until we (the authors) returned from Moscow. Because of the dislocations of the coup, however, when we arrived back in Leningrad Viktor was not to be found. He was baptized subsequently and has since become a leader among the believers in the city.

In retrospect, that simple worship service—on August 18, the eve of Russia's transformation—was also symbolic. It gave an eloquent answer to the aspirations of the Gospel Christians of the nineteenth century. It gave promise of a better day in Russia when the kingdom of God would find a central place in the hearts of multiplying numbers of Russia's citizens.

During the summer of 1992 we went back to St. Petersburg. The Saltykov-Shchedrin library's full collection of *The Christian* was examined with the aid of Ludmila Baronova, and an extensive sampling was photocopied. In the branch library on the Fontanka Embankment, all copies of the *Morning Star*, the fortnightly news magazine, were available for examination. What a thrill it was to see in the first number a letter to the editor from Leo Tolstoy, whose contention was that alcoholism was the number-one enemy and must be overcome through the application of an ethic based on the Sermon on the Mount. Arrangements were made with Lydia Loginova and Yuri

Dobrokhotov to provide the translations of selected items.

Then, on the 19th of April 1993, we made our way back to Moscow. Our intentions were the same as those of August 19, 1991. We were assisted by Elena and Olga, our talented teen age guides. Our first stop was the Lenin State Public Library of the USSR, as it was then designated, considered by the Russians to be the world's largest. This library had its beginning in the Pashkov Palace, which overlooks the Kremlin. The imposing structure (under total renovation at the time of our visit) was a gift to the state by Vasili Pashkov in 1862. At first, it housed the library of the Moscow University. Then it became Russia's first public library. Developed further, it received the Order of Lenin and its designation as the library for the Soviet Union. Modern buildings were added in the 1950s. Surely, in this significant repository, the story of Pashkov and his leadership of the Christians-Only movement in Russia would be chronicled!

Nothing. We searched the indexes. We consulted with the librarians. We received copies of the 125th anniversary commemorative booklet (1862-1987), but nothing surfaced on Pashkov or the movement he had shepherded. We searched farther afield at the Moscow State University library, the Library of Foreign Languages, the State Public Historical Library and at the historical museum bordering Red Square. The only response to our search was one librarian's comment, "This area has not been adequately researched as yet!" Clearly Pashkov was persona non grata, despite being one of Russia's wealthiest men and a friend of Tsar Alexander II. Though he had the distinction of having led the most significant Russian religious development in the nineteenth century, he had been exiled in 1884, early in the reign of Alexander III. His record had been expunged. Ironically, the official silence was an eloquent testimony to the significance of the man and his movement. In his day, as we had learned through the research of the University of Waterloo historian Edmund Heier,[3] Pashkov had engendered a major response from significant figures in Russian social, intellectual and cultural life, as well as Orthodox leaders. By the numbers it attracted, the arresting content of its teaching, and the spiritual vigor of those who espoused its simple, biblical practices, the movement was truly revolutionary.

Our Moscow visit in 1993 witnessed banners flying across the city streets, several proclaiming, "Christ is Risen," and others, "Vote in the Referendum, Vote for Freedom." A referendum on the leadership of the president was scheduled for the following Sunday, April 25th. Our travels included a brush with President Yeltsin as he passed within a few feet of us on his way to address a group of businessmen. Russia was changing, but economic prosperity had not caught up with the move toward democracy and a free market. Would the people look beyond present deprivations to a stable, prosperous and accountable future? Would the newly found freedom of the people for public religious expression go hand in hand with the rediscovery of biblical Christianity?

Our last search in 1993 was conducted a few days earlier, in the land where many of the late nineteenth-century believers had been exiled—in Siberia. We left Moscow and made our way to Irkutsk because we had information about a group of Gospel Christians meeting in this city beside the great Lake Baikal in the early decades of this century. This group would have been typical of many similar groups scattered across Siberia, punished for no greater crime than their determination to worship God according to the Scriptures. We arrived in Irkutsk on April 22 at 2:30 a.m. The temperature was minus eighteen degrees Celsius, with piles of snow as remnants of a blizzard. We were met by Yuri and Alexander who, themselves, had just arrived back home from a long trip into China for radio equipment. Both he and Alexandra were excited to tell us that since Wesley's visit in Irkutsk in 1990, they and Yuri's wife had been reading the New Testament and had determined to become Christians.

Yuri had done some advance work in checking traces of the turn-of-the-century evangelicals, but without success. We visited the Scientific Library of the University of Irkutsk, housed in a building (built c. 1804) which had been the home of the governor of Siberia in the last century. Across the road and facing the Angara River was the 300-year-old State Historical Museum, one of the oldest in Russia. From these sources the best we could accomplish was to receive a promise from a librarian that she would research the area of our interest. She identified some awareness of the Gospel Christian movement. A scheduled meeting with the local Evangelical Christian-Baptist church, which has roots in the awakening, failed to materialize. Our visit's highlight was with a young woman named Yulia and her mother, Lydia. Yulia, an avid listener to WCBC programs, had earlier requested a Bible. She had written that the only Bible available to her in Irkutsk was one a man rented out for one ruble per hour. He would actually stand over her so that she would not read for more than the allotted hour! We were warmly welcomed. No, the Bible we had sent had not arrived. Delight illuminated her face when Wesley personally presented a copy to her!

One Bible had been delivered in a nation of people hungry for the Scriptures. The Word of God was alive in Russia, a nation waiting to be delivered. We knew more surely than ever that the Good News was the answer for the deepest longings of the Russian soul. Hear, then, the rest of our story.

---

[1] Broadcast on BBC Russian Service, in *Listener*, Feb. 15, 1979; quoted in *The Oxford Dictionary of Modern Quotations* (Oxford: Oxford University Press, 1991), 204.

[2] The book was the *History of the Evangelical Christian-Baptists of the USSR*, published in Moscow by the Union of the Evangelical Christian-Baptists.

[3] It was not until after our return from the 1991 trip that Dr. Heier's insightful work, written in Waterloo, came to hand, *Religious Schism in the Russian Aristocracy, 1860-1900: Radstockism and Pashkovism* (The Hague: Marinus Nijhoff, 1970).

PART TWO

2

one Hundred Empty places

One hundred places were set in the dining room of the palace on the Great Morskaya, Number 43. The princess and her co-hosts, several of the most distinguished of the nobility in all Russia, waited with anticipation for the arrival of their guests. The luncheon was intended to consolidate the progress of the five preceding days of the religious unity conference and set the tone for the remaining three. Yet something was not right. The delegates had failed to arrive for the morning's meeting, and now the time set for the luncheon had passed. Minutes stretched to an hour. No one arrived. The afternoon faded into evening. Finally, one of the guests, an Armenian, arrived. Breathlessly he announced, "We were all arrested!"

The day was April 6, the year 1884. The city was St. Petersburg. The event was the gathering of one hundred Russian evangelicals. They had come at the invitation and expense of Colonel Vasili Pashkov and Count Modest Korff. Included were leaders from among Russian Baptists, Stundists, Mennonite Brethren, Molokans, and Dukhobors from the Ukraine and the Caucasus. The seventy out-of-town delegates were lodged in a hotel through the hospitality of Colonel Pashkov. Their luncheon on this particular day was to be provided by the recently widowed Princess Lieven, the former Countess von Puhlen. Also present to welcome the guests was the famed Dr. William Baedeker.[1] As well as a bountiful repast, the gathering would be a spiritual feast which would contribute to the objectives of the eight-day meeting. The purpose of the conference was to encourage unity among the Bible-centered evangelicals of Russia.

The Armenian reported, "We were treated as revolutionaries and our belongings searched. All the police could find were our Bibles and notes we had taken concerning the Scriptures." Indeed, at the heart of this confrontation was the Bible. These men were truly revolutionaries-of another kind. They sought heaven's mandate. If matters came to a choice, they would obey God rather than man.

Konstantin Pobedonostsev, Chief Procurator of the Holy Synod of the Russian Orthodox Church, was satisfied that this movement was dangerous to the state, the Church, and even to the Tsar. Considering the movement of which Pashkov was a leading influence "a vital enemy of Orthodoxy," he had called for the arrest of the evangelical delegates. In his mind, this group was little different from the political revolutionaries who were determined to bring down the empire through violence and assassination. The entire delegation was removed from the hotel, imprisoned, interrogated, and on the second day bundled off to trains and sent home. "You have no right to be here!" they were told.

In short order, Pashkov and Korff were expelled from Russia, sent into permanent exile. Their society for the distribution of Bibles and teaching materials was shut down. All known leaders of the evangelical groups were taken into custody. Public meetings of the "sectarians" were forbidden. Pobedonostsev sponsored the following twenty years of the most severe repression of Russian dissenters to the state church.

During the twenty years leading up to that fateful day in 1884, the spread of the Bible in the Russian vernacular had caused such dramatic growth in the evangelical forces that the authorities felt compelled to take this drastic action. In the examination of the events leading up to the April 1884 arrests and the ensuing fates of the Russian evangelicals, what unfolds is one of the most significant developments in Russian social and spiritual history. The accomplishments of Russians who, regardless of the consequences, placed their confidence in a vital relationship with Christ and the authority of the Scriptures, stand as a record of great inspiration. They had a remarkably clear vision of a united assembly of believers who would be Christians only. They knew that in their hands they held the keys not only to the kingdom of God on earth, but to a healthier and happier Russia.

The following sketch of Russian religious and social history leading up to 1884 will be familiar to many. The place of the word of God and the evangelical awakening, however, have been obscured by the torturous and absorbing events which surrounded the October Revolution and the movement's seventy years of exile in the wastelands of communism. Pashkov's record was all but expunged by his enemies when he was exiled—and this by imperial forces before the revolution. The anti-religious fervor of the Bolsheviks which resulted in the deaths of countless leaders and followers-Orthodox and Evangelical alike-the destruction of their properties, and the throttling of their activities, was also effective in blotting out from the minds of succeeding generations the significant histories of their spiritual forebears. This work will join with a growing body of studies which seek to return to the people of the former Soviet Union the stirring record of their past.

In order to understand the events of 1884 it is necessary to have some sense of the history of the Bible in Russia, of previous efforts to reform the religion of the people, and of the conditions which fomented social unrest in the nineteenth century. We turn now to the fascinating religious and social history of the Russian people.

----

[1] See Robert Sloan Latimer, *Dr. Baedeker and his Apostolic Work in Russia* (London: Morgan and Scott, 1907).

3
The Bible in Russia

The Bible came to Russia in the tenth century in the care of the Church. The Bible came to the hearts of the Russian people in the nineteenth century through the evangelical awakening. With the opening of the Bible for the Russian people, the "other revolution" began.

Christianity in its Eastern form entered Russia as a result of the energies of two brothers: Cyril (d. 869) and Methodius (d. 885), Greek missionaries who evangelized the border areas of the Slavic lands. Tradition has it that before the brothers left Constantinople, Cyril had devised a script, the Glagolitic, for writing the vernacular Slavic language. They began a translation of the gospels that may have been the first reduction of Slavonic to writing. "Their followers, St. Kliment and St. Naum, created a Slavic alphabet, later called Cyrillic, and in 886 established the first seat of Slavic higher learning in Ohrid [in present day Macedonia]."[1] With this beginning, Slavs living farther east received the works of Christian literature in what was later to be known as "Church Slavonic," "the basic literary language of Russia until late in the seventeenth century."[2]

Prince Vladimir, of Scandinavian extraction, was ruler of Kiev and areas of southern Russia (980-1015). He was influenced by his grandmother Olga and his wife, a Byzantine princess, both of whom had embraced

Christianity. Upon his acceptance of Christianity in 988 A.D., Vladimir required that his people receive baptism.

Conversion to Christianity and the evolving church organization were forcibly carried out by the prince in the teeth of resistance not only on the part of pagan priests but also of various strata of the population. Metropolitan Ilarion of Kiev admitted that the baptism of Kiev was forcible: "No one resisted the prince's order pleasing unto God, and everyone was baptized—if not of their own free will then out of fear of the giver of orders, for his religion was connected with power." The resistance to the replacement of the traditional cult was all the stronger in other cities. In Novgorod, the legend has been preserved of the introduction of Christianity there by Bishop Ioakim of Korusm and the prince's generals, Dobrynya and Putyata, "Putyata baptizing with the sword and Dobrynya, with fire."[3]

The Christianization of the Slavs by compulsion rather than by conversion would have serious consequences in later history as the Church remained an adjunct of the state for over nine hundred years.

Vladimir considered both the Church of Rome and the Eastern Church centered in Constantinople and then chose the latter. His emissaries to that city were taken by the beauty of its church architecture: "The Greeks led us to the buildings where they worship their God, and we knew not whether we were in heaven or on earth.... We know only that God dwells there among men, and their service is fairer than the ceremonies of other nations." Byzantine-style cathedrals were built in the cities of the eastern Slavs. Not only was holy architecture important but great attention was paid to the aesthetic appeal of a liturgy that enacted the "divine drama." The beauty of the paintings and the icons in church and home stirred the heart to worship. Mystery was emphasized, for heaven was beyond anything but vague perceptions of glory and wonder.

The preservation of orthodoxy (*pravoslavie*, "true praising"), a principal emphasis of Byzantine Christianity, was continued in Russia. The ordering of Christian doctrine according to the findings and pronouncements of the seven ecumenical councils, rather than simple adherence to biblical statement, was the foundation of the Eastern Church. With the acceptance of this focus, it is not surprising that there were no complete versions of the Bible produced in early Russia. "Most of the twenty-two surviving manuscript books from the eleventh century and of the eighty-six from the twelfth were collections of readings and sermons assembled for practical guidance in worship."[4]

The oldest surviving Russian manuscript, the Ostromir Gospel (1056-57), includes readings from the Gospels prescribed for church services and arranged according to the days of the week. The first printed Bible in Russia was completed in the late 1400s, the "Bible of Gennadius," which was based on translations from the Latin Vulgate of a number of Old Testament books and accomplished by Latin-trained associates of Gennadius of Novgorod. The Ostrog Bible of 1576-1580, the first complete Slavonic Bible, was based on Gennadius's translation. Later, Simeon Todorsky, an Orthodox theologian who became a pietist, produced "the most complete version of the Bible yet to appear in Russia," the Elizabeth Bible of 1751.[5]

A critical theology was not developed by Russian Orthodoxy. Rather, theology was to be defined by the lives of the saints. True piety could be achieved only in the ascetic life of the monastery. Christianity was to be seen, marveled at, and experienced in its mystery, more so than to be lived out in practical devotion. Precise doctrinal definition was rejected as a result of the vanity of human reason. Humble acceptance was the highest virtue. While the Bible was revered in Eastern Orthodoxy, and while theoretically it was the original source of correct observance, the writings of the church fathers were given an equal, if not greater, voice in determining faith and practice. While the Bible's stories were familiar through the dramatizations of the liturgy, its pages were not largely open to the people until late in the nineteenth century.

The Bible also came to Russia in the baggage of western European expatriates who arrived to live and trade in Russia. Those who came as Protestants were free to worship according to their customs and to expound the Scriptures to each other, but it was not permitted to extend these activities to their Russian neighbors. As citizens, the Russian Orthodox faithful were not permitted to change their religious allegiance. Russians, particularly those who were attracted to the West (as distinguished from the Slavophiles who resisted Western ways) were naturally open to the biblical emphasis of these groups. The Westerners' prosperity, sober life-style and piety impressed the Russians. Inevitably, the barriers were breached, and Russians began to sample for themselves the treasures of the word of God.

The Baltic regions of Livonia and Courland, present day Latvia and Estonia, had been penetrated by Lutheran teachings. When these regions succumbed to the armies of Ivan IV ("the Terrible," 1533-84), many Estonians, Latvians and Germans were deported in slavery to Asia, taking Lutheran doctrine with them. Later, these outposts would spread the influence of the Bible-centered German Pietistic movements which developed both at Halle and Herrnhut. The increased primacy of the Scriptures among Lutherans would subsequently have a potent influence upon the Russian people.

Further, the Bible came with Germans who immigrated to Russia. Catherine II ("the Great," who reigned 1762-96), of German ancestry, in 1763 invited German settlers to take up land in the south. Among some 25,000 colonists who accepted the invitation were Lutherans, Mennonites, and Pietists, for whom the Scriptures were paramount. Between 1764 and 1768 one hundred four colonies of German farmers were established along the Volga River in the Saratov area. An outstanding colony of the Unity of the Brethren was founded at Sarepta in 1764. In 1817, a number emigrated from Württemburg to the Russian province of Georgia, served by missionaries from Basel, Switzerland. The Germans' respect for the word of God would not be ignored by their Russian neighbors.

With the passing of the centuries, the Bible, exalted as God's holy book in its Church Slavonic form, remained largely incomprehensible to most of the people. With the dawn of the nineteenth century came an unexpected imperial interest in the New Testament. The tsar's awakening to the Bible had a remarkable impact on the shape of European politics and also laid the foundation for the Russian spiritual revolution.

When his ailing father, Paul I (1796-1801), was murdered, Alexander I became tsar and reigned from 1801 to 1825. As a child Alexander, at his grandmother Catherine's request, had been tutored by the wife of General von Lieven of Estonia, a Protestant. Upon Alexander's coronation, he appointed as his Chief Procurator of the Holy Synod Prince Alexander Golitsyn (1773-1844). From a respected Russian noble family known for its affection for things French, Golitsyn was at first a lover of the Encyclopedists, the French rationalists. At first he resisted the tsar's posting, but soon he became enthusiastic for his responsibilities. He decided to read the New Testament for the first time. Moved by the life of Christ and his teachings, Golitsyn was inspired in ways he had never experienced in

Orthodoxy. It appeared to him that the German pietists in the land were the better representatives of Christianity. In 1810, he was appointed administrator for the affairs of foreign denominations. This entailed his resignation as chief procurator but actually expanded his field of religious activities.

Tsar Alexander, at Golitsyn's encouragement, read the New Testament from Golitsyn's own Bible, also for the first time. The Tsar experienced a spiritual transformation. Alexander continued to read the Scriptures as he traveled through the newly conquered Finland during the summer of 1812. He was especially moved by the prophetic books of the Old and New Testaments. "A new world is opening up before me," he said. Golitsyn encouraged him, in his conflict with Napoleon, to make the Bible a kind of manual for the "spiritual mobilization" of Russia. The Tsar attended prayer meetings and Bible readings at services arranged by Golitsyn. Alexander began to interpret current events in view of the Scriptures and developed his own idea of "inner Christianity." He envisioned that somehow he might heal the wounds of religious division and create a brotherhood of "biblical Christians."[6]

Alexander followed the advancing Russian troops and the retreating Napoleon in a journey rather like a pilgrimage. He read the Bible daily, visited the Moravian villages in Livonia and at Herrnhut, attended Quaker meetings in London and celebrated the Easter liturgy at Paris. Between his first entrance into Paris in 1814 and the defeat of Napoleon at Waterloo in 1815, a movement developed which saw Alexander as the prophetic Man of Destiny. With the acceptance of this vision and the belief that the end of the Napoleonic wars was the beginning of a new day, the Tsar promulgated the Holy Alliance of September 1915, the "Christian answer to the French Revolution." Protestant, Catholic and Orthodox rulers, the majority of Europe's monarchs, pledged themselves to base their entire rule upon "the sublime truths which the Holy Religion of our Saviour teaches." They declared that "the precepts of justice, Christian charity and peace...must have an immediate influence on the councils of princes and guide their steps." The name "Alliance" was taken from the book of Daniel, and the Alliance was dedicated to the Holy Trinity. As the various countries united into "one family," there would follow "the treasures of love, science, and infinite wisdom."[7] While the vision was superior to the political debasement and self-serving national responses which followed, it was nevertheless indicative of the power of the Scriptures for shaping new inspiration for a tired Europe.

Alexander had delayed his departure from St. Petersburg—in pursuit of the retreating Napoleon—in order to meet with the English leader of the British and Foreign Bible Society. The Tsar's intent was to establish a Bible society for Russia. On December 6, 1812, the day Napoleon started by sleigh from Vilnius in order to escape from Russia to Paris, Alexander signed the decree. He and his two brothers became patrons of the St. Petersburg Bible Society. Golitsyn, now Minister of Cults and Public Education, was named president. The founding meeting of the Society took place in January 1913. Representatives of various domestic and foreign churches were present.

Bible societies had sprung up in almost every Protestant country following the establishment of the British and Foreign Bible Society on March 7, 1804. The Bible Society in Russia was the first in any Orthodox region. The first members of the Society were St. Petersburg pastors and international laymen. Its early—primarily Protestant—leadership expanded to include Orthodox and even Roman Catholic clergy, and chapters spread across the country. The Society's name was changed in 1814 to the Russian Bible Society. Golitsyn's original intention was to print Bibles only in foreign languages, but during its first two years it expanded to include Russian language translations as well. The Holy Synod continued to print the Bible in Church Slavonic, and the Society distributed and sold them at reduced prices. When Alexander visited London in 1814, he said to a delegation from the British and Foreign Bible Society that he regarded the Bible Society as "a most beneficial institution and one particularly necessary in Russia."[8]

On his return to Russia, the Tsar indicated his desire for a modern Russian translation. While the Tsar's request offended some, the Holy Synod sought to comply. On the translation committee was Archimandrite Filaret, a friend of Golitsyn, who was later to become the Metropolitan of Moscow. The New Testament was completed in modern Russian in 1819. By 1823, the Society had produced the Psalms as well as complete Bibles and portions of the Scriptures in Finnish, Karelian, Estonian (two dialects), Georgian, Armenian, Turkish (two dialects), Samoyed, Cheremiss, Chuvash, Persian, Kalmyk, Buryat, Tatar (three dialects), and Bulgarian; eighteen languages in all—"a tremendous achievement." Significantly, the Society was funded chiefly by a group of Russian nobles.

At the same time, opposition grew. There were those who revered the Slavonic as sacred, and all other renderings of the Scriptures were viewed as "wicked profanations." The reactionary Nicholas I (who reigned 1825-1855) closed the Russian Bible Society in 1826. "Enough Bibles have been printed," he said. Yet the influence of the Bible would not be stopped. In the same year, the twenty-year-old Scottish colporteur John Melville began his sixty-year ministry of distributing Bibles throughout Russia. During his lifetime he not only distributed thousands of copies of the word of God but often taught with a nondenominational perspective from the Scriptures. Because of work and that of others like him, the evangelical movement in Russia would be essentially a Bible-based movement.

A more liberal spirit returned with the coronation of Alexander II (who reigned 1855-1881), nephew of Alexander I. The young Tsar turned away from the suppression of the Bible's circulation by his father. In one of his earliest actions, Alexander II issued an 1856 edict which called for the translation of the Scriptures into modern Russian. Upon the 1867 completion of the Old Testament, he stated:

> In 1856 when I assumed the Imperial Crown, the Holy Synod, at a conference held in Moscow, deliberated on the means of spreading the word of God in the most abundant manner among Orthodox Russians, and recognized the necessity of translating...the books of Holy Scripture in the Russian language.... I pray to God that he will manifest the sanctifying power of his Holy Word for the progress of the Russian people in faith and piety on which rests the true happiness of empires and nations.[9]

In 1858, Alexander reopened the Russian Bible Society and in 1863 permitted the British and Foreign Bible Society to return to Russia to take up large-scale work. By 1867, the first time the complete Bible became available in the Russian vernacular, the Bible was circulating among literate Russians. Bible reading spread, and many began to think independently of the interpretations of the Church. A climate was created which nourished the evangelical awakening in Russia during the 1860s and 1870s. Historian Edmund Heier observes, "The reading of Scriptures, it must be remembered, was the very life of the new religious revival."[10]

The experience of Count Korff illustrates how the minds of even official Russia had become open to the influences of the Bible. In 1867, Count Modest Korff, Lord Chamberlain of the Emperor, attended the World Exhibition in Paris. There he happened upon the display sponsored by the British and Foreign Bible Society and was pleased to see copies of Russian New Testaments freely offered. The officials pressed three thousand copies of the Gospel of John upon him and urged that he distribute them in Russia. He expected that the Holy Synod would refuse permission to circulate them and was surprised when agreement was given. He had no difficulty in giving away the lot. Nothing revolutionary was intended by this. Korff merely believed that the Bible would have a positive effect among the Orthodox faithful. Soon considerable sums of money were forwarded by the British society for the purchase of Russian Bibles to be circulated without charge. In 1870, Korff was asked by the British Society to build a pavilion in the St. Petersburg Industrial Exhibition. Again, Korff was surprised when the Holy Synod gave not only permission but also funding. A total of 62,000 Bibles were given away! Each member of the royal family and its entourage received personal copies. Interest spread, especially among the noble families in the capital city. Private Bible studies began to be held in the homes of the upper class. Spiritual interest awakened.

The evangelical awakening in Russia was the early fruit of the circulation of the Bible in the language of the people. In turn, the distribution of the word of God across the land became a primary objective. So successful was this initiative that with the collapse of seventy years of militant atheism in the twentieth century, a lingering national hunger for God's word would become eloquently evident. As Communism crumbled, a great cry arose from the spiritually starved: "Give us Bibles!"

---

[1] Priit J. Vesilind, "Macedonia: Caught in the Middle," *National Geographic* (Washington: National Geographic Society, Vol. 189, No. 3, March 1996), 127.

[2] James H. Billington, *The Icon and the Axe: An Interpretive History of Russian Culture* (New York: Vintage Books, 1970), 5.

[3] Alexander Preobrazhensky, ed., *The Russian Orthodox Church, 10th to the 20th Centuries* (Moscow: Progress Publishers, 1988), 8.

[4] James H. Billington, *The Icon and the Axe* (New York: Vintage Books Edition, 1970, Random House, Inc., 1966), 7-8.

[5] Billington, 85, 108, 277.

[6] Billington, 282.

[7] Billington, 283-84, quoting W. Phillips, *The Confederation of Europe* (London, 1920), 301-2.

[8] Peter von Goetze, cited by Brandenburg, 29.

[9] Edmund Heier, *Religious Schism in the Russian Aristocracy, 1860-1900: Radstockism and Pashkovism* (The Hague: Martinus Nijhoff, 1970), 81.

[10] Heier, 81.

4
Reformation

The introduction of the Bible into the common language of a people typically has explosive results. This was true in the second and third centuries when the New Testament canon was completed and the Scriptures were circulated throughout the Grecian world in their original *koiné* or "common" Greek form. This was true in the fourth and fifth centuries when, translated into the "vulgar" (common) language of the Latins by Jerome, access to the Bible spread throughout the Roman empire. Early translations—Syriac, Coptic, and Armenian, for example—brought the word of God into the heart languages of other people. With the translation of the Bible into German, Luther laid the foundation for the great "protest" against Roman Catholic Christianity, which was perceived by many to have lost its way. Several renderings of the Bible in the maturing English language culminated in the 1611 "authorized" version of James I of England. This version not only enriched the English language but strengthened the Anglican choice of the "middle way" between Catholicism and Protestantism. Among both German- and English-speaking people, free access to the Bible in their mother tongues nourished further movements such as the Anabaptists and the German Pietists. Among English Evangelicals and Pietists a number of "restoration" attempts arose which sought to return to New Testament teaching.

The evangelical awakening in Russia, sparked by the spread of the Scriptures in the Russian language, was just as dramatic. Unlike the Western Reformation, reform in Russia did not have to deal with widespread religious division. Indeed, the earliest efforts at reform were to return to what was perceived to be a purer Orthodoxy. Later efforts were for a more modern Orthodoxy. In the West, the religious conditioning was strongly rationalistic, but in the East, emotion and mysticism were the characteristic elements. Yet reform in both regions turned to the Scriptures and, significantly, reached similar conclusions. The Russian evangelicals, in what developed into a distinctive reform movement, captured the vision of a Christianity centered solely in the authority of the Bible and of Christians united under the lordship of Christ. Inevitably, the evangelicals differed with the established Church, which followed, in addition to the Bible, the traditions of Orthodoxy. It is also true that the evangelicals did not always agree with each other. Consider that these had to deal with chaotic change, newly-emerging literacy, and social revolution, not to mention national isolation and regional diversity. The evangelicals' genius, however, was in the insights and accomplishments they gained in their attempts to practice primitive Christianity and to propagate this faith in Russia.

The uniqueness of Russian Orthodoxy, and therefore of subsequent reform activities, is rooted largely in three events which isolated the Slavic faith. First, the great schism of 1054 divided Christendom into Eastern and Western segments. Subsequent efforts to bring Russian Orthodoxy into a more compatible relationship with Roman Catholicism failed. And while traditions and practices of Orthodoxy and Catholicism are often quite similar, Russian Orthodoxy went on to work out a separate life. Second, the fall of Constantinople to the Turks in 1453 had the effect of severing Russia from Byzantium and its spiritual roots. Even though Russian Orthodoxy was called the "Greek Orthodox Church in Russia" until the twentieth century, Russian churchmen came to consider Moscow as the third Rome. Inevitably, the Russian Church followed an independent path. And third, the invasion of Russian lands in the thirteenth century by the Mongol hordes effectively isolated Russia from the West for three-and-a-half centuries.

The Mongols, with leaders such as Genghis and Batyi Khan, raided old Russia from the east. Kiev was sacked in 1240. One substantial claim is that Russia provided the buffer against Mongol invasion of Western Europe. That being true, the entire world is different because of what Russia suffered in those centuries. Yet the cost to Russia was isolation from Europe for much of the evolving medieval period. In spite of the Mongols' barbarity, they did respect the sanctity of the churches. Here the people found safety and moments of peace in the midst of the turbulence and suffering of their lives. Thus the people became deeply attached to the Mother Church of Russia. During the period of domination by Mongol overlords until its conclusion in 1590 with the final defeat of the Mongols, the kingdom of Muscovy gradually developed, with Moscow at its center. Accordingly, the Church's power came to be centered in Moscow where the leading churchman, the Metropolitan, took the title of Patriarch in 1589. The Orthodox Church in this period experienced a remarkable expansion. The vigor of the Church was directly linked to the development of the Russian monarchy, whose rulers professed to be Christians and viewed themselves as leaders and protectors of the Church. This further strengthened the bonds between state and church.

Contact with the West was never completely extinguished. Trade connections were maintained with the Hanseatic League, and Western heresies arrived through this linkage. Two contrasting responses were made to the emerging heterodoxy: the application of force or the appeal to biblical truth. Joseph of Volokolamsk (d. 1515) was a leading advocate of the use of force. The Tsar (the Russian title taken by Ivan IV in 1547, aping the ancient Roman usage "Caesar") was appointed by God, it was held, to rule the land. Since he had divine power, he must rule strictly with respect to spiritual matters. Orthodoxy must be protected with force. Heretics should be executed. The traditions of the fathers had equal authority with the Bible. Joseph believed that any indulgence in human opinion was "the second fall."[1]

On the other hand, monks in the Volga district, led by the abbot Nil Sorsky (d. 1508), believed that the proper response to heresy was an appeal to the authority of the New Testament "against which all other writings were to be measured."[2] There should be separation of church and state. Heretics should be dealt with in gentleness and in prayer. These monks resisted the many new canonizations of saints. They advocated freedom of thought and love in the place of outward ceremonies. In the end, force and tradition won out over gentleness and New Testament authority. A glimmer of hopefulness was extinguished, leaving behind "evangelism" by coercion and foreboding for the future.

Various movements of dissent arose during the intervening centuries of Russian church history. In the West, dissent was stirred through fresh investigations of the Scriptures with a view to greater freedom for doing God's will. In the East, dissent arose out of respect for the past, regard for established authority and reverence for the traditions of the fathers. One group, however, attempted to bring radical change to Orthodoxy. These were the *Strigolniki* (from *strigol*, "to shear," the occupation of their leader, Karp, a sheep shearer) who appeared in 1370. They protested against the inadequacy of the Orthodox priesthood. Priests and ordination were rejected. All brothers could preach, and all were spiritual priests. The sacraments were set aside. While the movement's leaders were either imprisoned or killed, the influence of the sect lived on. Generally, however, the reform process tended to turn people back to the original source, the Bible.

The attempt to reform Orthodoxy in Russia, not unlike reform efforts elsewhere, had the effect of spawning division. So steeped in the vision of an inviolable orthodoxy were the faithful that attempts to correct departures and corruption were often viewed as innovations and emendations. In 1551, the Synod of "the Hundred Chapters," the *Stoglav*, by the instigation of Makary, Metropolitan of Moscow, a follower of Joseph of Volokolamsk, had sanctioned the existing liturgy. Yet when it came time to print the ritual for the first time, the variations and uncertainties of the text surfaced. Leading in the revision was Nikon (1605-1681), who became Patriarch in 1652 and regent for the second tsar of the Romanov dynasty, Alexei. Nikon viewed himself as the "Great Sovereign" and attempted to function in a style similar to the Roman popes. Under his rule, the sermon acquired a completely new significance in the service. He founded a school for Greek and Latin, published a book of canon law, the *Kormchaya*, and fought for a greater independence of the Church from the Tsar.

Nikon's thorough-going reform of the ritual was sanctioned by the synods of 1666-67. Reaction, however, to these changes brought about the *Raskol*, "the rupture," in 1667. The great schism produced the "Old Believers," the *Staroveri* or "true believers." The Raskolniki were fearfully persecuted for their insistence that the new ritual was the doctrine of the Antichrist. At issue was the preservation of the long standing forms: the sign of the cross with the correct number of fingers, direction of the processions, the spelling of the name of Jesus, how often to repeat the Hallelujah, the number of loaves on the Lord's Table, the shape of the cross, and other concerns of Orthodoxy but not of biblical Christianity. The Old Believers rebelled against the "innovations," even though these changes were intended to restore to their original purity the ancient traditions of the Orthodox Church.

When the Old Believers separated from the state Church, no bishops became involved, but a number of priests participated in the schism. Eventually, the question arose with respect to the replacement of those priests who died. The schism split further into two groups: those who maintained the priestly order (the *Popovsty*) and those who functioned without priests (the *Bezpopovsty*). The latter, first organized in 1691, believed that the Antichrist had come, and they dropped all sacraments except baptism. They appointed elders, expounded the Scriptures and heard confessions among themselves. At the same time they maintained the traditional fasts and venerated icons and relics. The Schism, in fact, had the effect of driving many back to the study of the Scriptures and to an early attempt at primitive worship. The anticlerical posture would have echoes in the nineteenth century.

As time passed, the Old Believers fragmented into a number of movements which in turn created an atmosphere conducive to further division. Sectarian divisions such as the mystical People of God (the *Khlysty*, or "Flagellants"), known for their ecstatic dancing, and a further offshoot, the *Skoptzi* ("self-castrators"), followed the Raskol. Identified as the "rational sects" were the Dukhobors and the Molokans.

The Dukhobors ("spirit wrestlers") came into prominence in the later years of the eighteenth century. Attracting the lowly of Russian society, they repudiated the Orthodox Church. They believed that God dwells in each person but gives special blessing to some. These could attain to the stature of Christ in their own time, for Jesus was only a man. The New Testament age belonged to the Holy Spirit, they believed. They gathered without priests to sing Psalms and comment on selected Scriptures. They rejected baptism by water and were noted for their morality and industry. Stressing mutual love, they maintained a community of possessions. The Dukhobors believed in one invisible church of God and that they were its visible representatives.

The Molokans, or "Milk Drinkers," received this nickname because they drank milk during Lent, contrary to Orthodox practice. Their origins are obscure; they were first mentioned officially in 1765. These "Spiritual Christians," as they preferred to be called, made the whole Bible their sole rule. They rejected the sacraments, ceremony, the priesthood, the veneration of icons and saints, and refused military service. They believed the only true worship was worship from the heart, which is the temple of God. They rejected water baptism for baptism of the Spirit. They confessed to each other, held love feasts and, in place of an annual Eucharist, often broke bread in contemplation of the words of Jesus. The Molokans followed an allegorical interpretation of the Scriptures which gave rise to considerable diversity in opinion. They met only in houses under the leadership of a presbyter for prayer, singing of hymns, reading the Bible, and discussion of spiritual themes. They maintained a high morality and tended toward communal activity. Because they flourished, they were deported in 1823 to the Caucasus. The Molokans were forerunners of the evangelicals and became a source of membership as the new movement gained momentum.

Patriarch Nikon had been frustrated in his attempt to free the Church from the domination of the state and to make the patriarch more important than the tsar. Peter the Great (who reigned from 1682 to 1725), however, intensified the state's hold on the church. The reforms of Peter had the effect of more completely subordinating the Church to the will of the state. When the patriarch died in 1700, he was not replaced. In 1721, the office was closed, and in its place Peter established the Holy Synod, which was to be chaired by a chief procurator appointed by the tsar. Through the Synod, reform was carried out to the tsar's satisfaction. He attempted to take over some of the judicial functions of the Church. State administration of some church and monastic lands was imposed and their revenues diverted to the government. Religious duties of the laity were mandated. The number of clergy was restricted. While the education of the clergy and their families was improved, the Church was to remain aloof from the affairs of state. Always, Peter's orientation was westward. Impressed with German Pietism, Peter expressed confidence in August Hermann Franke of Halle and had Halle's works translated and circulated in Russia, as well as Johann Arndt's books on "True Christianity." These actions, as well as Tsar Peter's reforms, stirred both Slavophile reaction and conservative yearnings.

The first half of Alexander I's reign gave encouragement to the possibility of liberal reforms, both in government and in the church. In his later years, however, Alexander turned to mysticism and reactionism. After seven years as Minister of Religious Affairs and Public Education, Golitsyn was dismissed in 1824. The chief procurator became a minister of the government, increasing secular dominance over the Church. During the reactionary reigns of Nicholas I and later of Alexander III, "the Church had become the bailiff of the state and the state police were the executive organ of the Church."[3]

Those in power struggled to assure the Church's position of respect, authority and monopoly. Indeed, this was Pobedonostsev's ambition. Yet Orthodoxy was resistant to reform, locked in ritual, and diminished by division. Its priesthood lacked respect among the common people and was ignored by the nobility. The Church seemed impotent before the mounting social and spiritual problems of Russia, yet it demanded primacy of place in society. Another sectarian outburst could not be tolerated. The final upstart, Evangelicalism, would be rigorously suppressed and eradicated. Orthodoxy would unify the state through its spiritual leadership, bring reverence to the monarchy as its champion, and maintain the right praise of God for all the people.

The simple act of turning to the Scriptures in the latter half of the nineteenth century in Russia by nobility, the peasants, and the emerging middle and industrial classes was not at first a protest against nor a demand for reform within the state Church. The desire to learn God's will firsthand was sincere and non-threatening. However, the authorities were scandalized that untrained and unauthorized people would directly access the Scriptures. Their reaction, overdrawn and unseemly, transformed the simple activity into a vigorous reform movement, especially as discrepancies between traditional practice and biblical precedent became evident. The movement passed beyond the reform of the Church of tradition to seek the return of the primitive church of the New Testament.

---

[1] See Hans Brandenburg, *The Meek and the Mighty: The Emergence of the Evangelical Movement in Russia* (New York: Oxford University Press, 1977), 8.

[2] Brandenburg, 8.

[3] Brandenburg, 47.

5

Revolution

The nineteenth century was a period of turmoil, tension and disappointment for the Russian people. Extended periods of conservative reaction alternated with brief periods of liberal advance. Traditional forces were committed to consolidating the three realities of Russia: Orthodoxy, autocracy, and nationalism. On the other hand, modernization was sought by many of the aristocracy, by the emerging intelligentsia, and by the growing classes of bourgeoisie and laborers. The implacable stance of the imperial authority and its supporters, which included the Church, was met by a revolutionary response from reactionaries among the people. While revolution was not successful on the broad scale until early in the twentieth century, its foundations were laid during the nineteenth. Religious revival during such a period of discontent was an alternative response to the troubles but was vulnerable to misunderstanding and abuse. Such was the experience of the Russian evangelical awakening.

A burgeoning Russia which had continuously added to its territory since the fourteenth-century days of the Kingdom of Muscovy was at war throughout the nineteenth century. Several defeats, however, signaled that the empire was either overextended or inadequately governed. The interminable warfare had two consequences: crushing burdens upon the people and growing dissatisfaction with the structures of government.

Much of the struggle focused on conflicts among Russia, the Balkans, and the trans-Caucasus Muslim states. Russia was also at war with France from 1805 to 1807, a war which she lost. In the years 1806-1812 she was at war first with Turkey and then with Sweden. In 1812 Napoleon invaded Russia but was repelled. The Russo-Turkish War took place in 1828, broke out again in 1853 as the Crimean War, and resumed again in 1877. From 1858 to 1860, military campaigns pushed eastward to the Amur River, and the northeastern Caucasus region was finally taken. Tashkent was captured in 1865 and Khiva overcome in 1873. Such continual warfare, with all the resources necessary for putting armies in the field, feeding them, and supplying them with arms, subjected the general population to great stress.

The nineteenth-century rulers, for all their power, were captive to the forces which had shaped Russia. They seemed incapable of an objective appraisal of the complications and unable to launch effective solutions to the problems which wracked the state. The Russian monarchy's belief in the "divine right of kings" persisted long after the West had abandoned the concept. Awareness of social and political reforms in the West raised expectations among some citizens while Slavophilic reaction urged the rejection of these ideas and a freezing of Russian traditions. As the century concluded, revolutionary forces were the more determined while the reactionary voices which counseled the Tsar were the more strident.

Alexander I promised reform upon his accession to the throne in 1801, stirring hope that some progress would be made in resolving the social problems of Russia. Alexander demonstrated concern for the lives of citizens and the burdens of war. "Thousands who had been removed and banished without trial were returned. Russians received permission to journey abroad, foreign books were admitted once more, and the ban on private printing presses was removed."[1] Alexander was preoccupied with the problem of serfdom and considered various reforms. He was unwilling, however, to challenge the interests of the landowners. At the same time, he opposed any solution which might require compulsion. Taxation had been heavy throughout these early years of the century. Now, with Alexander's attempts to withdraw from the battlefield and focus on problems at home, he learned just how desperate the conditions were. Some wars had been fought by Russia with the help of foreign gold because the nation's resources were utterly depleted.

Alexander's later years proved to be reactionary. In frustration, certain of the aristocracy who had been emboldened by Napoleon's defeat began to dream of a new Russia. They held a vision in which the nobility and able people would participate in a constitutional monarchy. A gathering at Senate Square in St. Petersburg on December 14, 1825, the day of the coronation of Nicholas I, ended in tragedy. At the end of the day, cannons were fired into the crowds. The slaughter of the "Decembrists" set in motion forces of rebellion and revolution which continued until the Revolution of 1917. It marked "the beginning of this tremendous process which was to end in global convulsion." One historian observed, "From that point Russia was like an overheated boiler on which all the safety vents had been sealed up." From 1825 on, a host of conspiracies were fomented by assorted nihilists, anarchists, and social revolutionaries, until the victory of Lenin and the Bolsheviks was realized.

The aristocracy was impatient with imperial intransigence. It was also disillusioned with the sterility of the Church. Characteristically devout, many of the nobility found little spiritual stimulation in the formalism of Orthodox ritual. The state's subordination of the Church, intensified by Peter's disdainful treatment, contributed to the detachment of the nobility from the Church. The imperial wish was for the sons of the aristocratic families to enter the military or government service, not the priesthood. As a class, the priests were viewed as ill-trained, poorly educated, and suited to leading only the common people. At the same time, a deep sense of longing coupled with despair moved the aristocracy to seek a spiritual answer. Some found it in a renewed devotion to the Church, mediated especially through monastic "elders." Others turned to those voices which urged a fresh examination of the Scriptures and a personal quest for Christ.

Nicholas I ruled with an iron hand from 1825 to 1855. Not only did he shut down the Russian Bible Society; he suppressed Protestant missions among non-Orthodox in the Transcaucasus. His appointment of Protosov as Chief Procurator initiated a series of conservative leaders of the Holy Synod, of whom Pobedonostsev was the crowning representative. Russia's defeat in the Crimean War (1853-56) shortly after Nicholas's death signaled the beginning of the end of the old Russian order.

Serfdom was by no means the only problem of Russia; it was only the most universal social issue. It was the "red flag" which represented other enormous burdens endured by the people. Alexander Herzen, one of the nobility who was sympathetic to the peasant's plight wrote in a private letter:

> The peasant who has been acquitted by the court trudges home no more elated than if he had been condemned. In either case the decision seems to him the result of capricious tyranny or chance. In the same way, when he is summoned as a witness he stubbornly professes to know nothing, even in the face of incontestable facts. Being

found guilty by a law-court does not disgrace a man in the eyes of the Russian peasant. Exiles and convicts go by the name of unfortunates with him.... Between the peasantry and literature there looms the monster of official Russia. "Russia the deception, Russia the pestilence," as you call her. This Russia extends from the Emperor, passing from gendarme to gendarme, from official to official, down to the lowest policeman in the remotest corner of the Empire. Every step of the ladder, as in Dante, gains a new power for evil, a new degree of corruption and cruelty. This living pyramid of crimes, abuses and bribery, built up of policemen, scoundrels, heartless German officials everlastingly greedy, ignorant judges everlastingly drunk, aristocrats everlastingly base: all this is held together by a community of interest in plunder and gain, and supported by six hundred thousand animated machines with bayonets. The peasant is never defiled by contact with the government of aggression; he endures its existence only in that is he to blame.[2]

Alexander II began his reign under the shadow of the Crimean setback and understood that a new epoch had arrived. In the beginning, he was reform-minded, even as his uncle had been. The 1860s were known as the "Epoch of the Great Reforms." Alexander emancipated 22.5 million serfs in 1861. He instituted trial by jury in 1864. A provision for limited local self-government was made for the provinces in 1864 and for the cities in 1870. Reforms also came to the financial system, military affairs, and censorship in 1865. Throughout Alexander's reign the educational system was steadily expanded and improved. As has been noted, he encouraged the nation to turn to the Scriptures. For these moves, Alexander won the title "Tsar

Liberator." Following an attempt on his life in 1866, however, Alexander turned away from reform. Still, on the day of his assassination—March 1, 1881—he had secretly approved an arrangement by which leading members of the public would be included in the machinery of his government.

Alexander's reforms did not bring satisfaction. While serfdom was eliminated, both peasants and landowners were unhappy with the changes. Many peasants found themselves to be in a worse plight than before their freedom. Unable to initiate a positive response, they found ways to punish the society which dealt with them so cruelly.

> The Russian peasantry, emancipated from slavery only a few decades before and still suffering from socio-economic consequences, fell into murder, robbery, desecration and lawlessness the minute it felt the government's knots loosen.... In the countryside, and often in the towns, they smashed the landowners' estates to pieces, pilfered any remaining movable property indiscriminately, tortured the rich for their hidden money, and released the "red rooster," that is, set fire to every thing. They burned libraries and dug out the eyes of their masters' horses with nails. At times it was impossible to distinguish "left-wing" from "right-wing" pogroms.[3]

A growing number of educated persons, including the emerging intelligentsia and those of the "bourgeoisie," an expanding middle class of commercial wealth, sought a place in Russian society. Turning from traditional values and institutions, many came together in the "Populist" movement. A concern for the improvement of the human condition stirred these groups to seek radical solutions to the problems of society. Nihilism became the new religion for many. Revolution and anarchy were the answers given by desperate, if intelligent, hearts.

Industrialization generated a third class: the laborer. Many of these were agricultural workers forced off the land. They left one hardship for another form of exploitation which was even more severe. "Most workers lived in factory-owned barracks, in common 'dormitories' with double- or triple-decker berths. Three or four families huddled together in the corner of a small room."[4]

Schemes for social utopias were advanced. The Russian "Sunday School" movement of 1858-62, which attempted to bring education to the poor, was the first of several large-scale penitential efforts by urban intellectuals. In 1873-74, an outpouring of concern and conscience resulted in "the trek to the people," in which several thousand upper-class Russians went out to the villages and rural areas to live and work with the peasantry. Alexander's authorities reacted, however, and 770 were arrested. Even the poor reacted negatively to the trek, being suspicious of motives and disliking the "foreign ideas" introduced. Many became disillusioned with the Populist movement and turned to terrorist organizations. Assassinations were committed in the name of "good will to the people."[5]

Ironically, one of the assassins of Alexander II claimed at his trial, "The essence of the teaching of Jesus Christ...was my primary moral incentive." In fact, the moral teachings of Jesus were popular even though his deity and the supernaturalism of Christianity were rejected by many of the intelligentsia. Atheism spread among the intellectuals. Many supporters of the new, materialistic atheism were sons of clergy and students of theology, reflecting a failure of the Church. D. S. Mirsky observed, "The sons of the clergy were especially prominent among the new men of the sixties.... If he was the son of a priest, he would of necessity be an atheist."

Alexander III (who reigned 1881-1894) assumed his throne in a wave of reaction, purges, and repression. The Tsar's killers were hanged. The educational system, identified as the source of the radical ideas, was restricted and censored. Religious dissent, which would weaken the Church and thus the monarchy, was vigorously suppressed.

This was the temper of the times in which the fateful convention of Russian evangelicals was conducted in 1884. The social and political reaction to the Tsar's assassination swept up the evangelical movement in its suppressive net and dealt it undeserved punishment, casting the evangelical awakening as a variation of revolutionary thought and subversive action. Much energy was expended by the state toward stamping out this "sectarian" movement. Evangelicals were called on to shed their blood for Christ. Their battle tactics, however, were love, long-suffering and unswerving faith. These non-threatening dissenters became true revolutionaries of another kind!

[1] Charles Raymond Beasley and Nevill Forbes, *Russia from Varangians to the Bolsheviks* (London: Clarendon Press, 1918), 354.

[2] Edward Crankshaw, *The Shadow of the Winter Palace: The Drift to Revolution, 1825-1917* (London: MacMillan, 1976), 287-289.

[3] Boris Shagin and Albert Todd, eds., *Landmarks, A Collection of Essays on the Russian Intelligentsia, 1909* (New York: Karz Howard, 1977), xliii.

[4] Andrew Rothstein, ed., *History of the Communist Party of the Soviet Union* (Moscow: Foreign Languages Publishing House, 1960), 20.

[5] See Igor Shafarevich, "Socialism in our Past and Present," *From under the Rubble*, Alexander Solzhenitsyn, ed. (Boston: Bantam Books, 1976), 24-65.

6
Evangelical
Beginnings

As the nineteenth century progressed, the necessary ingredients for a spiritual revolution emerged. A sterile Orthodox Church, compromised from its inception with entanglements in a "kingdom of this world," was an empty option for the nobility, alienated from the intelligentsia, and without answers for the peasantry. At the same time sectarian dissent was multiplying, often with bizarre results as people conferred with their own feelings, fears, and fads. Belatedly, Russia opened to the industrial revolution and the advancing culture of the West. The heightened expectations of the people were frustrated by the determination of the state not only to preserve but to intensify the dominance of imperial rule. In reaction, materialistic ideologies were spawned which readily fed radical minds but which were patently empty of moral and spiritual values. Their ends could be gained only through revolution and internecine struggle.

Deep in the soul of Russia, however, was a yearning for God's peace and the abundant life offered by Jesus Christ. Bursting into this darkness came the promises of Christ, read for the first time by the people from the pages of Scriptures written in their vernacular. With this unfolding, the other revolution began. This revolution was opposed at first through imperial intransigence and vested ecclesiastical interests and later by the revolution of viciousness and atheism. Together, these represented a hundred years of despicable persecution and unthinkable suffering for people whose only aim was to know God directly from the pages of his revealed word. The arsenal of these spiritual revolutionaries contained the weapons of meekness, piety, faith, hope, and love. Their revolution ultimately triumphed, for the Empire and communism have both fallen under the judgment of history. Russia's only remaining hope is that she will visualize and attain the promises first proclaimed by these gentle, faithful revolutionaries.

It became more common as the century advanced for defenders of the state Church, in their efforts to suppress growing dissent, to cast the evangelicals as converts to foreign Protestant movements. This played to the spirit of nationalism and to the innate xenophobia of the Slavophiles. It ignored, however, the diversity of peoples and faiths which the growing Russia encompassed. It also overlooked the fact that the evangelical movement quickly captured the interest of growing numbers of Russians who developed their own responses to the gospel. The evangelical Christians, particularly, developed as an indigenous movement within Russia.

The nation was fortunate in that it was spared an exposure to the full gamut of Western Protestant sectarian division. Rather, those Westerners who had the greatest influence in Russia were an enlightened group motivated by pietistic and evangelistic revivals in their respective homelands. Included were Lutheran Pietists, German Baptists, Anglican Evangelicals, Moravian Brethren, and Mennonite Reformers. These had a common confidence in the primacy of the word of God and were energized by a personal awakening to God's message. In fact, Russia was favored in those days by the best that the West could offer.

The times were full in Russia during the 1860s. It is significant that, two years after the emancipation of the serfs in 1861, the British and Foreign Bible Society returned and went vigorously to work. The British society in turn bolstered the efforts of the Russian Bible Society, which had resumed its efforts a full seven years earlier. In 1867, the Old Testament was delivered in the language of the common people, making the whole Bible now available. In the decade of the 1860s, military successes were enjoyed and social reforms took place. Improvements were made to the legal system, education, the financial system, and municipal government. Encouraged but still unfulfilled, simple Russians reached out to the word of God. In southern Russia and the Ukraine the movements of the Stundists and the Russian Baptists were born. In the capital region in the 1870s, developments took place which prepared for the rise of the evangelical Christians.

Stundism began as a movement among pietistic Lutherans in Germany early in the nineteenth century and was carried to Russia by German settlers during the time of Nicholas I. Pietism, with its emphasis upon an active faith and a pure life, moved away from the elaborate Lutheran ritual to a simpler practice. This revival may be said to have begun with Phillip Jakob Spener (1635-1705) of Frankfurt. Spener charged orthodox Lutherans of his day with superficiality. He formed small, devotional gatherings, the *collegia pietatis*, for Bible study and discussion. Spener is well remembered for his work *Pia desideria* (1675), which called for the widespread circulation of the Bible among the people. His student was August Herman Francke, whose influence in the University of Halle helped to spread Pietism throughout Germany and beyond. A chief characteristic of Pietism was its claim to be founded exclusively on the Bible. Unlike Lutheranism, which was bound by creeds, the Pietists held to a faithful return to the Bible and the careful application of scriptural truths. The appeal was to turn away from cold dogma to "true Christianity," the title of a book by Johann Arndt. A more popular form of Pietism developed in the province of Swabia in the duchy of Württemberg, where the practice developed of conducting Bible studies at set hours, or *Stunden*. The name "Stundist," a name given at first in derision, was transferred to Russia as a foreign word and came to describe the Russian expression of the German Pietists.

The German Johannes Bonekemper (b. 1795) was trained in the Swabian tradition of the Pietists. Upon his ordination, he traveled to the German colony at Rohrbach near Odessa in Russia to take up his ministry in this village and in six nearby German settlements. Rohrbach had been founded in 1810 when various Germans emigrated from Alsace, the Palatinate, Baden, and Württemberg. Both Reformed and Lutherans joined to form a "Protestant" congregation. After several years of little progress—the community seemed indifferent to spiritual matters—Bonekemper scheduled a *Stunde*, and a spiritual awakening followed among the German settlers. Soon a hundred members were active. A conflict arose, however, when the formal Lutheran service was imposed, and Johannes was forced to leave Rohrbach. His son, Karl, was able to carry on his father's work. Fluent in Russian, Karl extended his activity to include Russian language meetings with harvest workers who had been attracted to the German *Stunde*.

Among those Russian peasants who participated in the Rohrbach Stunde were Ivan Ryaboshapka and Michael Ratushny. These young men returned to their villages and set up *Stunden* among their Russian countrymen. Ryaboshapka (b. 1832) came to the village of Lyubomirka in about 1857 to work as a shepherd and two years later hired out to a German miller, Martin Hübner, who was a believer. Ivan was twenty-seven when he bought a Russian New Testament. He confessed to Hübner, "If I were to follow this book, I would have to change my whole life." The miller replied, "Ivan, either this book becomes the basis of your life, or else you perish because of it."[1] Soon a *Stunde* of some twenty Russian men was active in Lyubomirka, of which Ryaboshapka and Maxim Kerachenko were leaders. Ryaboshapka became one of the most successful evangelists of the early Stundists. With his newfound conviction, he roamed the surrounding steppes preaching, "I once walked in darkness, but I have seen the light." By 1870, *Stunden* had begun in eleven nearby villages through Ivan's leadership. In Lyubomirka by that year, there were one hundred forty Stundists meeting and in the whole district of Elizavetpol, two hundred twenty-four.

Michael Ratushny (b. 1830) was a *muzhik*—an illiterate serf—who lived in the Russian village of Osnova, near Odessa, in the time before the freeing of the serfs. While working for Germans in Rohrbach, where he became a foreman, he was encouraged to study a Russian New Testament. Michael, then in his twenties, learned to read for this very purpose. Michael "felt a burning desire to understand God's words with his own mind and to explain them to others." [2] He became a successful farmer, owning a large farm with a stone house, horses, and oxen. With Ryaboshapka, he also became a roving evangelist. A Russian *Stunde* was established in Osnova, possibly as early as 1860. Participating in the *Stunde* was Ivan Onishchenko, a migrant worker who also had served the German settlers. In 1866, the St. Petersburg press reported a "new sect" of Stundists in south Russia.

The Stundist movement spread to other centers. Vitinkov Balaban (b. 1832) joined the harvesters from Chaplinka, south of Kiev, and was associated for a time in 1867 with Ratushny in Osnova. He returned to Chaplinka to secure a passport and stayed to found a *Stunde* there. Also in this area, the District of Tarashcha, were peasants in the village of Ploskoye who had been exposed to Bible studies during their harvesting trips. These gathered in 1868 to read the Scriptures in the home of the peasant, Pavel Tsybulsky. Within a year, this man was arrested.

Near the village of Lyubomirka was Karlovka. Here a group of Russian peasants were influenced by German Baptists in an adjacent German colony, Alt-Danzig. Ten peasants broke with Orthodoxy to form a Russian Baptist congregation. One of its leaders was Yefim Tsymbal. A Mennonite Brethren leader named Abraham Unger had baptized Tsymbal, who, in turn, baptized Ivan Ryaboshapka in 1870, the first Russian Stundist to accept baptism. Ryaboshapka then baptized Michael Ratushny in 1871. This conjunction of German and Russian Baptists, Mennonite Brethren, and Stundist leaders who accepted baptism is significant.

The Mennonite presence in Russia was one consequence of the several waves of Germans entering the empire: several thousand Mennonites were among the Germans who accepted the invitation of Catherine the Great to settle land in the Ukraine from 1789 to 1796. More followed from 1803 to 1809 in response to Alexander I's offer of land. Intense persecution in their homelands had spurred this resettlement. The Mennonites, who received official recognition in Russia in 1863, maintained a distinctly separate existence, their lives centered in their carefully ordered churches, schools and farming enterprises. The Mennonites' communal and insular ways restricted their contribution to the Russian evangelical awakening to example and encouragement. Yet their Russian neighbors looked on with respect and interest.

The Mennonites of Russia also experienced a revival in the mid-1860s. Eduard Wüst (1818-1859), a Pietist German minister, came in 1845 to minister to the emigrants from Württemberg who had settled near the Sea of Azov. In his fourteen-year ministry in the German *Stunden*, he preached a pietistic gospel and encouraged separation from all established religion. Wüst extended his preaching to include Lutherans, "Separatist" Lutherans, and Mennonites. As one result, a revival took place among certain Mennonites. These broke with the larger group to form the "Mennonite Brethren," who eventually began to practice believer's baptism.

An example of the influence of Mennonite Brethren on their Russian neighbors is found in the village of Sofievka on the Dneiper River, less than a mile from the Mennonite village of Friedensfeld. Among those Russians who were impressed with the Mennonite life and faith was Peter Lysenko. Semiliterate, he had managed to learn to read the Bible. Repeatedly, Peter asked the Mennonites to baptize him, but this was an illegal act and he was repeatedly rejected. Finally, in 1875, a Mennonite minister agreed to baptize Lysenko. For this action, Peter was thrown out of his father's home. The Mennonites helped him build a small house.

Baptism was not at first readily accepted by other Stundists. The Baptist leader, Johannes Oncken, founder of the German Baptist movement in Hamburg in 1834, had come to south Russia in 1869 and had encouraged the Stundists to accept believer's baptism and the ordination of their preachers. Vigorous debate arose among the Stundists concerning the place of baptism.

The baptism of leading Stundists, however, had two results. First, it signaled the Stundists' decision to separate from Orthodoxy. During 1870, other actions reflected this choice to the authorities: icons were removed to be stored in attics or delivered to the priest; the first funeral was conducted without a priest present.

With a growing sense of their independence, the Stundists began to shape their gatherings into simple congregations. Each congregation appointed an elder and a deacon as the attempt was made to model their groups after New Testament practice. The Stundists began to perform their own marriages even though the result was that their children were considered illegitimate by the state. Finally, they began to keep their own community records, taking over the function normally maintained by the state Church. These moves spurred the authorities from their tentative interference of the late 1860s to determined opposition in the early 1870s.

The second result of the baptism of Stundist leaders was the growing tendency of Stundists to merge with the Russian Baptists, who arose as a parallel movement. The existence of the Russian Baptists was the inevitable result of the German Baptist presence in Russia. The German Baptists had only newly arrived in Russia, though they had been in Poland since 1850, occupying territory later absorbed by Russia. German Baptists came to the Baltic regions of Latvia in 1860 and Lithuania in 1861. The first believer's baptism of a German settler took place in the German colony of Alt-Danzig on May 10, 1864. Shortly, some thirty other Germans followed suit.

The Russian Baptists mark their beginning with the preaching of the Prussian Martin Kalweit. A Lutheran who accepted the teachings of the German Baptists, Kalweit was sent by Oncken to Vilnius as a vocational missionary. Kalweit briefly led a German Baptist church in his home and then proceeded in 1863 to the Caucasus, where he began to work among the Russians, particularly the Molokans. His first Russian convert was Nikita Voronin who was baptized in the Kura River near Tiflis (now Tbilissi, capital of Georgia) on August 20, 1867. The historian Walter Sawatski identifies this act of baptism as marking "the official date for the beginning of the evangelical movement in the Russian Empire."[3]

A Molokan for whom baptism was not a familiar practice, Voronin had himself read the Scriptures and determined his need to be baptized. In turn, Voronin's early converts, in 1871, were also Molokans: the seventeen-year-old Vasili G. Pavlov (1854-1924) and the twenty-five-year-old Vasili V. Ivanov-Klishnikov (1846-1919). Voronin was "determined that the smug Molokans should also become New Testament Christians."[4] After at least one hundred years of activity, the Molokans had become narrow and rigid. A revival among some Molokans developed from the unusual ministry of Yakov D. Delyakov. Nicknamed *Kasha Yagub* ("Jacob the Priest"), Delyakov was a Persian Nestorian who became a Presbyterian missionary and ministered to Russians! His converts became the "New Molokans." It was from among these that a number of the future leaders of the evangelical awakening arose. Included were Pavlov and Ivanov-Klishnikov who would become leaders of the Russian Baptists.

Voronin founded the first Russian Baptist Church in Tiflis in 1868. By 1876, this congregation had forty members. The second Baptist congregation was organized near Novo-Ivanovka in Elizavetpol, also in the Caucasus.

Kalweit was eventually expelled from Russia because of his missionary activity among Russian nationals, and Pavlov became the recognized leader of the Russian Baptist movement. Pavlov's Molokan family lived in Vorontsovka in Georgia, then a vulnerable border region, to which they had been exiled by Nicholas I. At age five, Pavlov was reading the Bible in Church Slavonic in Molokan meetings. In 1870 at age fifteen, he found a small pamphlet which led him to faith and, the next year, to Voronin, who accepted him as an apprentice. At age twenty-one in 1875, Pavlov was sent to Hamburg to become a favorite pupil of Oncken. He was ordained as a Baptist preacher in 1876 and sent back to Russia. His gift for languages enabled his effective ministry in the multilingual Caucasus region. He was knowledgeable in some twenty-five languages including Russian, Georgian, Tatar, Armenian, Persian, German, Hebrew, and Latin. By 1880 he was preaching in Tiflis, unhindered by the authorities. Later, as a prominent Russian Baptist leader, he became a target for Pobedonostsev. Pavlov was instrumental in attracting Stundists to the Baptist movement.

The Russian Baptists continued under the influence of the German Baptists and were drawn into their system of ordination and church membership. This limited them somewhat from developing a fully indigenous Russian leadership. "By the time of Alexander III, the first Russian Baptist congregation was thirteen years old."[5]

The evangelical awakening in southern Russia thus began in the early 1860s, took shape as the decade advanced, and with the overreaction of the authorities gradually moved to a position independent of Orthodoxy. The first attempted assassination of Alexander II took place in 1866. His consequent sharp turn from liberal to conservative policies coincided with the beginning harassment of the evangelicals. Opposition continued to grow until a two-year lull, strangely enough, followed the successful 1881 assassination of the Tsar. The Russian Baptists, partially under the shadow of the German Baptists who were granted official status in Russia in 1879, were less effective in drawing the peasantry than were the Stundists and attracted less hostility from the authorities. Also, Russian Baptists evangelized primarily among the Molokans and were less threatening to the supporters of Orthodoxy.

The Stundists, on the other hand, became the early target for official repression: they were peasants, distinctly Russian, and increasingly disrespectful of the sacred symbols of Orthodoxy. At first, their gatherings were innocent efforts to study the newly accessible word of God without any intention of reproach to the Church of which, by accident of birth, they were members. Two factors, however, ultimately forced the Stundists' separation from the state Church. First, the discrepancies between the simple gospel and the encrusted ritual of the Church became increasingly evident as the movement grew more knowledgeable in the Scriptures. Second, the authorities mounted a strong response to the impertinence of these unlearned peasants who would presume to interpret the Scriptures without the aid of the village priest.

Early in the 1860s, the Russian Stundists were watched with interest and some uneasiness. Brandenburg reports the existence of official citations of these activities in the middle of the decade. On February 10, 1865, a Church document cites a meeting of seventeen men and three women in Ratushny's home in Osnova. Similar meetings had been taking place for the previous four years, it was noted. In April, thirty-two people gathered to read Scriptures and sing hymns. In October, a note of alarm about the "sect of the reformists" was registered. In February 1866 however, these people of Osnova were still attending the Russian Orthodox Church.[6]

Opposition grew from this point. At first, the civil authorities and the Church officers moved independently and somewhat unevenly. The *Stunde* of Ignatovka, a village near Osnova, was opposed by the villagers. Three families were evicted on charges of apostasy from the Orthodox Church, conversion to "reformed law" and "abuse of holy icons." Their two leaders were sent away to the army. Early in 1867, a rural Church leader investigated Stundist activities in three villages—Osnova, Ignatovka, and Ryasnopole. His report went to the bishop in Odessa and then on to the governor-general of the province. It was estimated that fourteen families, fifteen persons and five families in these villages respectively were participating in the Bible studies. The assessment was given, however, that these were merely pietistic circles gathered for mutual edification and could be tolerated. A priest reported that the Stundists had "affirmed with tears they had not abandoned the faith, that they recognized no new doctrine. They did not feel guilty because they met to read the Bible and sing. They would be happy to speak to the archbishop."[7] However, by the summer of 1867, the archbishop of Odessa concluded that the sect was dangerous. By the end of the year, a report was received by the governor-general which charged the Stundists with "communist principles." The tendency to see secret revolutionaries everywhere caused alarm in the Church, even though the number of perceived dissidents was relatively small.

Ryaboshapka was arrested in 1867 and again in 1868 and sent away to do penal labor. Later, he and his family were threatened with expulsion from his village, only to be saved by the intervention of the governor of the district. On one occasion when he was beaten for conducting an illegal meeting, Ryaboshapka said of the whipping, "It burned, yes it burned. But it was nothing to the fire of Jesus' love in my heart."[8] Ratushny, too, was imprisoned for reading the gospels; but while he was in jail, he found that all the prisoners wanted to read them!

The Stundists, in July 1868, appealed to the governor-general concerning the harassment they were receiving. The petition submitted was signed by Ratushny, Balaban and two others. "They are tormenting us because we read the gospel.... We want to live as Christians, and they want to make us stop this. But we will not reject Christianity. We want to live according to the gospel as it is written. And for this they harass us."[9] In 1869, Ratushny was placed under police supervision. In September 1870, the archbishop of Odessa, following an interview with Ratushny, requested "a legal penalty against the heretic." Balaban was arrested in May 1873 and again in October, charged with blasphemy against the icons and enticing Orthodox believers into the *Stunden*. He was sentenced to one year's imprisonment. Persecution in his town of Chaplinka was led by the police chief, Popov, who broke into homes, whipped those in whose houses no icons were hanging, and forcibly broke up the Bible studies of the Stundists. In the same year, Ratushny traveled to St. Petersburg to present a petition from the Stundists to the Tsar. The petition for relief from persecution stated that thirty-five persons were presently in jail as Stundists; it included one hundred six signatures from four villages.

In 1878, Ratushny, Balaban, and others were brought to trial and acquitted. Even yet, there was popular approval of the Stundists. They were seen to be sober workers, thrifty farmers, responsible taxpayers, and a pious people. Stundism had become a significant movement, having spread by 1880 to a dozen southern Russian provinces and several in the north as well. Years of opposition by Church and state had not succeeded in removing Stundism. To deal more positively with its threat, in 1880 at St. Petersburg an Orthodox lay fraternity was established. Its purpose was to compete with Stundism by advancing Orthodoxy. A publishing house was set up, and books, tracts, and sermons were distributed. "Missionaries" were sent out to speak against Stundism. Then the assassination of the Tsar took place. As the newly crowned Alexander III listened to the swelling chorus of reactionism, Pobedonostsev, appointed chief procurator of the Holy Synod, labeled the Stundists with a "socialist character." That was sufficient to call for their extermination.

---

[1] Hans Brandenburg, *The Meek and the Mighty: The Emergence of the Evangelical Movement in Russia* (New York: Oxford University Press, 1977), 82.

[2] The All-Russian Union Council of Evangelical Christian-Baptists celebrated in 1960 the centenary of Stundism in Russia (Brandenburg, 65).

[3] Walter Sawatsky, *Soviet Evangelicals since World War II* (Kitchener, Ontario: Herald Press, 1981), 27.

[4] J. C. Pollock, *The Faith of the Russian Evangelicals* (New York: McGraw-Hill Book Company, 1964), 63.

[5] Brandenburg, 98.

[6] Brandenburg, 66.

[7] Brandenburg, 72.

[8] Pollock, 62.

[9] Brandenburg, 76.

7

st. petersburg

St. Petersburg in the 1870s was a world far removed, both in distance and reality, from that of the peasants of southern Russia. Yet the word of God stirred the people of this imperial center as powerfully as it had those on the southern steppes. The city was the embodiment of the vision of Peter the Great. Its splendor outshone that of most European capitals. Its grand buildings were stamped with Italian and French design and were hung with the richest art the world could offer. Its citizens were open to Western ideas, but no thought energized them as did the word of God when it was opened to them in the mid-1870s. Many of the aristocracy were captured by its teaching, even to the point of creating a massive rift between the traditionalists and those who found in it a transforming spirituality. Through the nobility, the word of God was shared with all classes in a spontaneous, guileless outpouring of evangelistic enthusiasm. The egalitarian effect of the gospel saw the social merging of nobility, artisans, laborers, cabbies, and servants in the shared delight of the Scriptures.

The vigorous circulation of Old and New Testaments in the language of the people had been carried on by the British and Russian Bible societies for a decade. The biblical focus of two tsars, Alexander I of memory and the contemporary Alexander II, had not passed unnoticed. At the same time, all of the mounting frustrations of the empire were gathered into this ruling city. In its basements, the revolutionaries secretly built their bombs, marked their targets, plotted bloodshed, and lusted for destruction. In its salons, those who would lead the other revolution spoke openly of grace and freedom, of a new day of peace and union.

It is understandable, given the liberal climate which Alexander II at first encouraged, that even the Orthodox Church supported the distribution of the Bible in the 1870s. The complete Bible in the Russian vernacular was officially published and offered by the Holy Synod in 1875. The Church's positive response to Count Korff's circulation of the Gospel of John in 1867 and the prominence given to the offering of the Scriptures at the Industrial Exposition in 1870 have been noted earlier. These things could happen in a capital where sophistication and some degree of independence marked the aristocratic class. Even in the south it was not the circulation of Bibles which caused consternation among Church and state so much as who read them and with what effect.

There appears to be no direct linkage between the spiritual revival in the days of Alexander I and that during the reign of Alexander II. However, the availability of the New Testament in the common language since 1819 had its leavening influence even during the restrictive, thirty-year reign of Nicholas I. The evangelical awakening in St. Petersburg in the mid-1870s, which certainly echoed the earlier revival, was more than a superficial response to a novel occurrence. Only among the nobility of the imperial city could the enervating ennui have reached such depths. The ruling class was sated with self-indulgence, frustrated by regressive policies, disillusioned with their "trek to the people," fearful of the rising tide of discontent, spiritually hungry, and unfulfilled. Times were ripe for change, and change came. Described by Edmund Heier, the last half of the nineteenth century was "one of the most complex epochs of the development of Russian social, intellectual, political, and religious thought."[1]

> The loss of religious belief, coupled with a skeptical attitude towards any means of obtaining Russia's salvation, whether by government repression or rigorous application of Orthodoxy, liberal reforms, populism, or terrorism—all had been tried and found wanting—could only increase pessimism, disillusionment, and despair in an already chaotic, meaningless existence, a world without firm footing . It is out of this skepticism and incredulity, out of the impossibility of solving the problem of theodicy, and most of all out of a never-ceasing search for righteousness and truth, that a new spiritual movement found its origin among the upper classes.[2]

The religious awakening which occurred among the nobility and spread to the rest of Russia was repressed by imperial forces at first, driven underground by Communistic brutality later, and largely forgotten by current secular analysis. Still, it irreversibly conditioned the Russian nation. The seed planted and suppressed in darkness for over a hundred years is in the process of blossoming as the third millennium dawns. In the full blooming of the evangelical flower, the importance of the awakening in Russia in the 1870s will be fully appreciated. The spark that ignited the spiritual revolution in Russia was carried to St. Petersburg by an unusual figure: an Englishman known as Lord Radstock.

Granville Waldegrave (b. 1833) inherited the title Lord Radstock from his father at age 27. He was a product of the evangelical and pietistic stirrings in England during the 1800s and particularly the 1850s revival which touched such English aristocrats as Lord Russell, Lady Buxton and Earl Wemyss. Radstock was educated at Oxford, where he took double honors in history and science. As an officer of the British army, he went to the Crimean front at the end of the war. There he contracted a fever and was close to death. This experience set the course of his life; he would serve Christ. From 1860 on, Radstock gave his life to preaching and humanitarian efforts. He worked in prisons and hospitals, raised funds for homes for immigrants and hostels for women. He preached in the slums of London's East End and in the salons of the nobility. In these efforts, he spent a large personal fortune. He also ministered to his fellow officers at Aldersgate, but in 1866 he gave up his command so that he could give full attention to preaching the gospel. He enjoyed a successful ministry in the London suburb of Weston-Super-Marie, where responses were gained from four hundred people of social standing. Included was Dr. Baedeker, who became famous for his ministries across Russia. From 1867 to 1869, Radstock led fruitful revivals, conducted Bible studies in the drawing rooms of London's elite, and worked in mission halls and refugee centers.

Radstock was an Anglican of "Low Church" persuasion, but for a time he was under the influence of the Open Brethren, an offshoot of the Plymouth Brethren, led by John Nelson Darby. The Brethren were noted for their dispensationalism, their determination to restore New Testament Christianity through trust in the absolute authority of the Scriptures, and their rejection of ecclesiastical organization These emphases would show up in Radstock's preaching in Russia.

As a member of the Evangelical Alliance (a

worldwide association of pietistic believers formed in London in 1846), Radstock attended an international conference in Holland in 1869. From there he traveled to Paris and, being fluent in French, carried on his preaching ministry. It was here that he met women of the Russian nobility, including a grand duchess and the princess Elizaveta Chertkova. The princess was grieving the loss of her two sons and her husband, the general adjutant to the tsar. Both of these ladies made new commitments to Christ under Radstock's preaching. They in turn invited him to Russia. Indeed, Radstock had a concern for Russian spirituality. When he met Russian noblemen in Paris, he would ask them if they would pray for their country. He added the names of those who agreed to do so to a list which he kept in his Bible.[3]

It was not until five years later, at age forty, that Radstock reached Russia. He arrived in St. Petersburg during Holy Week in April 1874 and began a six-month ministry which was to have remarkable results. He traveled to Russia, undeterred even by word of his mother's death. At first, he confined his activity to the American Chapel and a German Lutheran church, facilities used by various expatriate believers. Soon, however, at the invitation of his friends among the nobility, he moved his preaching to the drawing rooms of the palaces of the city. Within a short time, his meetings were attended by "an enormous mass of listeners."[4]

Radstock was a driven person. In England, his constant preaching brought him close to collapse. In St. Petersburg, he maintained a schedule of up to fifteen hours a day, speaking at least twice and conducting personal discussions throughout the day. He chose to walk from appointment to appointment so that he might hand out New Testaments as he went. His teaching was

done in French, a second language for many of the
aristocracy. Radstock's preaching was centered
exclusively in the Scriptures. He avoided any reference
to Orthodoxy or to the denominations. His approach
was simple, his manner modest, and his sincerity
evident. His high credentials and his unassuming spirit
made him highly appealing to the Russian nobility.

The public services that Radstock conducted
began with a silent prayer in which divine guidance
was sought. Then he would read a passage of Scripture,
followed by a spontaneous comment upon the selected
text. The main point which emerged from the selection
would be mentioned repeatedly. Radstock had been
impressed, during a visit to the United States, with the
repetition used in American advertising, and he
consciously followed this example in his preaching. He
would conclude, following several hymns and a prayer,
with an invitation to his hearers to "find Christ."
Personal appointments were then encouraged and
scheduled.

Lord Radstock was an immediate sensation in
St. Petersburg. A hunger for spiritual food not satisfied
in Orthodoxy was a major factor, as well as the
aristocracy's interest in things Western. Radstock's
biblical focus, however, opened the hearts of the people
to the word of God; the flame that ignited the other
revolution. Dostoevsky, in his *Diary of a Writer*, recounts
his first contact with Radstock a year before his arrival
in St. Petersburg.

> I found nothing startling. He spoke neither
> particularly cleverly or in a particularly dull
> manner. But yet he performs miracles over
> human hearts; people are flocking around him,
> many of them are astounded; they are looking
> for the poor, in order as quickly as possible to

bestow benefits upon them; they are almost ready to give away their fortunes.... He does produce extraordinary transformations and inspires in the hearts of his followers magnanimous sentiments.[5]

Radstock's teaching included a mix of the Protestant emphasis upon "faith alone," English pietism and the Open Brethren's stress upon a nondenominational position. The Brethren, including such men as George Müller, held to the absolute authority of Scripture and a nonclerical approach to Christianity. In keeping with this orientation,

> [Radstock] interpreted the gospel independently of any religious affiliation or close ties with any sect. His deep interest and contact with members of various creeds opened up new perspectives and provided him with renewed courage and strength. He visualized the possibility of uniting them through a common use of the Scriptures and the great love for Christ. This concealed mutuality of spiritual sympathy and oneness he wished to make a living realization.[6]

Perhaps unwittingly, Radstock, in his nondenominational emphasis, touched a responding chord within his Russian audiences. A contemporary of Radstock was V. Solov'ev, a leading Russian religious philosopher, who saw Russia's mission as bringing about the union of the churches. He spoke, in his *Unification of All Christendom,* of his desire for spiritual oneness in the world in a perfect society where the state would be subjected to Christian principles.[7]

Radstock's pietistic leanings led him to require the experience of salvation to be accompanied by personal holiness. "This holiness teaching opposed all state church activity because the true church was

thought to be entered by faith, not simple membership
in a local church."[8] Radstock placed great importance
upon the work of the Holy Spirit. He believed that, while
he opened human hearts to the word of God, it was the
Holy Spirit who would convict the listeners of sin and
bring them to belief. Radstock's offer of free grace in an
Orthodox setting, where salvation was linked with good
works, alarmed priests in the city, who believed that
such preaching would lead to licentious living.

Radstock's message was simple and steadily
repeated: salvation through the atoning death of Jesus,
salvation open to all. He believed in baptism and the
Lord's supper, in one faith, in one church of Christ, and
in the Bible as the only authoritative text. Good works
were encouraged, not to gain salvation, but because of
gratitude for the salvation which had been received. All
should be "just Christians," he held, united in a
Christian brotherhood in which all were equal.

The popularity of Radstock, which spread
quickly throughout the aristocratic community in St.
Petersburg, was accomplished without showmanship,
charisma, intellectualism, or overpowering eloquence.
Instead, Radstock was respected for his modesty,
generosity, and genuineness. His sincere interest in
people and in the Russian nation communicated
powerfully to his hearers. Chiefly, Radstock was
uniquely positioned to supply spiritual nourishment for
those who hungered and thirsted for righteousness.
Many of the wealthy and powerful of St. Petersburg
flocked to hear him. His widespread influence is
identified by a comment from Archbishop Butkevich,
who said of St. Petersburg society in the late 1870s, "Not
to be a Radstockist meant to lower oneself in the eyes of
society and risk the danger of being labeled a backward
person. To take exception with the teaching of the
English lord in a private home was considered equal to

insulting the host."[9]

Those who accepted Radstock's teaching did not consider themselves to have removed from the Orthodox Church. Yet gradually they saw themselves as "believers," "children of God," or *Evangelskie Christijanie*—"Evangelical Christians"—as distinguished from *Evangelicheskie*—foreign evangelical churches. For the followers of Radstock, spiritual renewal, rather than an altered church loyalty, was the goal. They sought deeper understanding of the word of God and, through this means, spiritual enrichment and a stronger faith.

Opposition did not come quickly even though foreign preaching to Russian Orthodox believers was prohibited by law. No doubt, the prominence of those participating in the city-wide revival retarded official reaction. Radstock's first visit to Russia lasted only six months. By the time of his return in 1875, it was perceived that the Radstock movement was growing at the expense of Orthodoxy. Predictably, among his followers there was a decline of interest in the rites of the Orthodox Church, particularly in the veneration of the Virgin and the saints. The Slavophiles saw this as a movement of Western Protestantism and objected to what they perceived to be a developing sect.

One leading aristocrat, prince Vladimir Meschchersky, who published the weekly periodical *The Citizen*, spoke out strongly against the movement, which he described as a "blasphemous sect." He appealed for the banning of the meetings and the expulsion of Radstock. In 1875 Meschchersky published a satirical novel, *Lord Apostle of High Society*, which was but a transparent ridicule of Lord Radstock and his followers. First published in installments in *The Citizen*, the completed production was distributed as a four-volume work in 1876. The protagonist, an "English Lord

Kitchik" (German for "gaudy"), was an irresponsible, opportunistic person of questionable morals. The unfairness of this characterization moved Dostoevsky, who had edited *The Citizen* during 1873 and 1874, to write, "What utter rubbish Meschchersky has churned out.... Simply rubbish."[10]

The misrepresentation also spurred the author N. S. Leskov to write *The Schism in High Society: Lord Radstock and His Followers*. This work was also presented serially in the pages of *The Orthodox Review* from 1876 to 1877 and in book form in 1877. Intended to be something of a defense of Radstock, the work complimented his person but was critical of his teachings as shallow and short-lived. Leskov, nevertheless, showed "keen interest in the movement and in its leaders" and "became the best qualified writer to speak of the new religious movement," which "he did abundantly in newspapers and periodical articles."[11] In 1878 in the *Religious Public Worker*, Leskov acknowledged that he had overstated his criticism of Radstock. Whether pro or con, the attention given to the evangelical awakening among the aristocracy during the period 1874-1878 indicates the considerable impact it was having upon St. Petersburg.

To remove himself as a focus of the growing reaction, Radstock voluntarily left Russia in 1876. Unwisely however, he published abroad an open letter to the citizens of Russia in which he described Orthodoxy as "a transitional state of Christianity." The reaction was considerable. Radstock then returned two years later, going to Moscow to minister, without success. Leo Tolstoy acknowledged his visit with a short description of the "self-styled missionary in Orthodox Moscow." Tolstoy had earlier questioned the sincerity of the aristocrats who followed Radstock, but he accepted the sincerity and spirituality of the man.

Finally, in 1878 at the height of the revival he had launched, Radstock was forced to leave Russia. He ministered subsequently in England, Sweden, Denmark, and elsewhere and died December 8, 1913 in Paris. Radstock had paid Russia only three short visits, but she would never be the same.

---

[1] Edmund Heier, *Religious Schism in the Russian Aristocracy, 1860-1900: Radstockism and Pashkovism* (The Hague: Martinus Nijhoff, 1970), 1.

[2] Heier, 25.

[3] See David Fountain, *Lord Radstock of Mayfield* (Southhampton: Mayflower Christian Books, 1984).

[4] Gregory L. Nichols, "Pashkovism: Nineteenth-Century Russian Piety" (master's thesis, Wheaton College Graduate School, 1991), 13.

[5] Fyodor Dostoevsky, *Diary of a Writer* (New York: Octagon Books, 1973), quoted in J. C. Pollock, *The Faith of the Russian Evangelicals* (New York: McGraw-Hill Book Company, 1964), 67.

[6] Heier, 32-33.

[7] Heier, 33.

[8] Nichols, 8.

[9] Quoted in Malcolm Jones, "Dostoevsky, Tolstoy, Leskov, and Radstockism," *Journal of Russian Studies* 23 (1972), 9. See Nichols, 26.

[10] Nichols, 27.

[11] Heier, 68.

8
christians only

A short distance from the tsar's winter palace, also facing the Neva River, was the palace of Colonel Vasili Alexandrovich Pashkov. Tsar Alexander II was Pashkov's friend and a frequent guest at gatherings in this home. Like most of the members of his social circle, the colonel knew of the English missionary, Lord Radstock. Pashkov's initial response to Radstock, not unlike that of several of his friends, was negative. In fact, Radstock's presence irritated him. One source for this emotion may have been the influence Radstock exerted in the life of Pashkov's wife, who had met Radstock earlier in England and who had responded readily to his simple message. Indeed, Pashkov would often leave a room when Radstock arrived! On one occasion, however, Radstock was present in Pashkov's home when the dinner hour came and was invited to remain. Politeness required that Pashkov be a good host. Conversation led to spiritual matters, and soon Radstock spoke of Paul's teaching on grace in Romans. Finally, Radstock invited the whole family to kneel in prayer, and Pashkov was smitten. His decision that night in 1874 would affect the heart of all Russia.

Pashkov (1813-1902) was born into one of the oldest, wealthiest, and most prominent families in Russia. He received the best education possible, loved the arts, and filled his several palaces with priceless paintings from around the world. He eventually became a captain in the cavalry, served as aide-de-camp to the emperor, and retired as Colonel of the Guard. Ironically, he fought in the Crimean conflict and, near death from a battle wound, made the same commitment that Radstock was making meanwhile in the opposite camp. Some twenty years later, his resolve took on a new meaning when he encountered Radstock and subsequently became "one of [Radstock's] most ardent followers."[1]

Pashkov was just one of a number of St. Petersburg aristocracy influenced by the spiritual awakening which resulted from Radstock's 1874 efforts. In fact, the first to respond was Count Modest Modestovich Korff, Lord Chamberlain of the emperor. He earlier had become the contact man for the British and Foreign Bible Society in the distribution of Bibles in Russia. Korff and Pashkov would become close spiritual confidants and active partners in the evangelical undertakings which followed. And together, they later suffered the inevitable reprisals.

Also challenged by Radstock's teaching was Count Aleksey Pavlovich Bobrinsky, Colonel of the Corps of Nobles and Minister of Transportation in the tsar's government. On one occasion, Radstock was a dinner guest at the invitation of Bobrinsky's wife. As was his practice, Radstock discoursed on the book of Romans. Bobrinsky quietly questioned his teaching. Excusing himself, he retired to his study where he began to write a refutation of the interpretations he had just heard. While rereading what he had written, he became convinced that he was in error and that Radstock was correct. "Like a sudden flash of light in my soul, I found that Jesus was the key, the Beginning and the End."[2]

Bobrinsky became "a living example of a repentant nobleman."[3] For the next twenty years of his life until his death in 1894, Bobrinsky dedicated his life and his holdings to the evangelical cause. A very able speaker, Bobrinsky became a vocal representative of the movement. Tolstoy, an associate of Bobrinsky, reflected his admiration for the nobleman in several writings. In February 1878, in a letter to Prince S. S. Urosov, he wrote, "[Bobrinsky] is a remarkable person...an ardent believer...[His words] provoked an envy of that greatness and peace which you possess."[4] Also in March 1878 he wrote to his aunt, A. A. Tolstaya, Lady in Waiting to the empress:

> At no time has anyone spoken to me so well about faith [as] Bobrinsky. He can not be contradicted because he does not set out to prove anything, he merely asserts what he believes and one feels that he is happier than those who do not possess his faith. Moreover, one senses that his happiness of faith cannot be acquired through the intellect but only through a miracle.[5]

A number of noble women of St. Petersburg were among the first to be moved by Radstock's ministry. Madame Elizaveta Ivanovna Chertkova, wife of the Adjutant-General to the Tsar, who had been instrumental in drawing Radstock to Russia, was the mother of Vladimir Gregorievich Chertkov, one of Tolstoy's closest associates, and sister to the Countess, Mrs. Vasili Pashkov. Madame Chertkova, as an evangelical, became active in a prison ministry where she successfully directed hardened criminals and political prisoners to Christ.[6] She joined with her sister, Mrs. Pashkov, and with Countess Gagarina in efforts which aided poor women and young girls by establishing sewing rooms to teach skills and generate income, as well as organizing district laundry rooms where girls were apprenticed. The sisters Countess Gagarina and Princess Lieven both opened their mansions for evangelistic meetings.

Princess Lieven, who was Russian Orthodox, and her husband, a German Lutheran, had both made spiritual commitments earlier while visiting England. Her husband, who died shortly after Alexander's assassination in 1881, had cautioned her that the path that she had chosen would lead her out of Orthodoxy. Her daughter Sophie wrote regarding her mother's earlier spiritual awakening, "The whole fullness of responsibility connected with being a Christian, she did not realize until later [through Radstock]."[7] Later in the century, when oppression had decimated the evangelical movement, Princess Lieven's faithfulness and open palace became the mainstay of the evangelicals in St. Petersburg.

One devoted follower of Radstock was Madame Maria Gregorevna Peuker who was for a time editor of *The Russian Workman* (1875-1886). This widely circulated publication, filled with devotional, ethical, and religious teaching, drew commendation from the Orthodox clergy, who even reprinted articles from it. N. S. Leskov, a noted writer whose numerous articles and works explored the religious developments of his day, at first criticized Peuker for importing much of the paper's contents from the Religious Tract Society of London and presenting the material without adaptation to the Russian setting. Subsequently he admitted his excess and, in fact, became editor of this paper during 1879. He wrote a stirring eulogy of Peuker's life when she died suddenly in 1881.[8]

The outstanding feature of the spiritual awakening in St. Petersburg was the holistic response of those who heeded its call. Colonel Pashkov, whose contributions to the movement resulted in the labeling of the evangelicals as "Pashkovites," directed his great wealth and full energies to the cause. He was considered to be one of the wealthiest men in Russia, with land holdings in Novgorod, Moscow, Tambov, and Orenburg, as well as copper mines in the Urals.[9] Pashkov became a devoted student of the Scriptures and in his own right emerged as a principal leader and spokesman of the evangelicals, along with Korff and Bobrinsky. Pashkov conducted Bible studies and prayer meetings in his home and organized similar meetings throughout the city. He personally visited prisons, factories, and hospitals, distributing Bibles and tracts wherever he went.

Pashkov directed his philanthropy in support of his Christian objectives. He opened a canteen in the Vyborg district of St. Petersburg, where inexpensive meals were served to students. The schools and universities exposed students to nihilism and atheism, but Pashkov's efforts provided a place where they were engaged in discussion on Christian themes. Pashkov worked out an arrangement with St. Petersburg University which permitted him to direct gifts of money, food, and clothing to any student who would sign a card indicating that he was an evangelical seeker. These students returned to the university armed with the knowledge of the Scriptures and with tracts and Bibles which they distributed to their peers. In the workers' district of St. Petersburg, Pashkov set up three free eating houses where thousands were served daily. These also became centers for the dissemination of his teachings. According to a certain Glebov, who opposed the evangelicals, these restaurants became a kind of "folk university" in which the "nonsense" preached by the speakers "became the essence of a creed, and people from every corner of St. Petersburg and the provinces flocked to these places where the new religion was proclaimed in simple Russian without Church Slavonic texts." He grudgingly admitted, "In this manner, Pashkov's popularity increases, for he is spoken of everywhere—in palaces and in peasants huts with the respect and honor befitting his personality."[10]

Pashkov was particularly concerned for the poor farmers who would leave their families and farms and come to the city during the winter months to work as cabmen and drivers. He set up tea rooms for them and supplied them with Bibles, tracts, and teaching. In the spring, they returned to their villages, armed with these materials and a new vision. While the movement began in the salons of the highest circles of St. Petersburg society, it soon began to reach into every level of the culture. The meetings in the palaces were open to all, and people from every walk of life attended. There was a conscious effort to remove all sense of class distinction. The antagonistic Glebov quotes the assertion of the aristocrats present at a meeting which he attended out of curiosity.

> Here prevails absolute equality and brotherhood; there are no gradations or ranks.... We have sinned along with our fathers for generations and it is time to cleanse ourselves of all evil.... As if the people are not equal, as if the same blood is not flowing in their veins...as if we were not all identical children of the Heavenly Creator.... This is our purpose for gathering here.[11]

The spiritual revival spread quickly among St. Petersburg nobility because it had a ring of genuineness. Since it fed a long suppressed hunger and was not merely an infatuation with the West nor a temporary dalliance with a novel experiment, the turn to the Bible and to an active faith captured convictions and redirected lives. Support for this assessment is found both in the egalitarian spirit which characterized the awakening, as noted above, and in the readiness of many among the nobility to devote whole fortunes to sharing the newfound faith.

The Society for the Encouragement of Spiritual and Ethical Reading (SESER) was established in 1876 by Pashkov's initiative and personal investment. It became the engine for the broad dissemination of the treasures of the simple gospel.[12] The Society of Pashkov, as SESER was also known, developed, according to Heier, "an enormous propaganda machine unparalleled in the Russian Empire at the time." Indeed, "the activities of the Society in the field of religion were so extensive and well organized that no other movement could have measured up to its potential as a force capable of transforming Russia on a religious, ethical basis."[13] The Society functioned for eight years before being closed down by Pobedonostsev in 1884. During that period several million pieces were published. Included were the Old and New Testaments in modern Russian, books, hymnbooks,[14] and the weekly periodical *The Russian Workman*, which was now funded by the Society and worked to advance SESER's objectives.[15] Over two hundred attractive pamphlets were printed, with several running into repeated editions. These were prepared specifically for the lower classes and circulated for a minimal charge when they were not given away. These found their way even into remote villages where literacy received a major boost because of the eagerness of the common people to claim the contents for their own. "The only reading material readily available were the Bible and the brochures of the Pashkovite Society. True, the Holy Synod's Bible had been available since 1878, but not so readily and at enormous cost, whereas the Pashkovite literature was mostly free."[16]

Initially, the work of the Society was approved by the Tsar and the Holy Synod, but the material published had to satisfy both state and Church censors. The materials circulated by the Society were moralistic, ethical and biblical in their emphasis and avoided any reference to Church doctrines or existing creeds. Many were translations from English and German pietistic sources. Original pieces were prepared by members of the Society, including Radstock and Pashkov. Also featured were writings of several renowned Orthodox leaders. Large quantities were sent to the Orthodox seminaries and to schools, and teachers and priests joined in circulating the writings.

Yet the spread of the evangelical movement did not depend solely on the circulation of the written word. The Russians were natural and instant missionaries when their faith was stirred. The Bible and prayer meetings in aristocratic homes were attended increasingly by people of all classes. These in turn shared their findings in their own circles. Those of the upper classes possessing country estates continued their teaching activities when away from the city during the summer months. Teachings spread throughout the surrounding villages. In the winter, those dubbed as "Pashkov intellectuals" by their detractors would fan out among these villages to continue the work done in the summer.

How significant was the Pashkovite movement in Russia? The attention paid to it by leading literary figures of the day gives some indication of its position. In the nineteenth century, Russian fiction became the avenue for the examination and promotion of social and religious ideas which were under restraint elsewhere. Russian literature of this era characteristically searched for spiritual truth. It expressed "a thirst for the salvation of the people, of humanity and the whole world, from unhappiness and suffering, from the injustice and slavery of man."[17] Edmund Heier, historian and professor of Russian literature, identifies the recognition of the evangelical awakening by leading authors of the day. In the introduction of his previously cited work, *Religious Schism in the Russian Aristocracy, 1860-1900:*

Radstockism and Pashkovism, he states his premise that
the awakening spurred by Radstock and Pashkov was
"first...a unique phenomenon of Russian religious and
social thinking, and second...a literary motive in the
belles lettres of nineteenth-century Russia." He lists such
"profound religious thinkers and writers" as Tolstoy,
Dostoevsky, Leskov, Boborykin, and Meschchersky
among those affected by the movement.[18] Not all
fictional reference to the evangelical awakening was
positive, and frequently its leaders were caricatured and
slandered. However, this attention increased knowledge
of the movement, and often curious readers became
converts.

The "Golden Age of Russian Prose" climaxed in
the works of the two greatest representatives of Russian
fiction—Fyodor Dostoevsky (1821-1881) and Leo
Tolstoy (1828-1910). Dostoevsky plumbed the depth of
the human psyche in his great novels *Crime and
Punishment* (1866), *The Idiot* (1869) and *The Brothers
Karamazov* (1880). Tolstoy was moved by spiritual, social,
and moral concepts in works considered to be among
the world's greatest: *War and Peace* (1869), *Anna Karenina*
(1877) and *Resurrection* (1899).

Dostoevsky was a true Slavophile. He believed
that "Orthodoxy is the best and truest faith; a Russian
not professing Orthodoxy cannot be a Russian."[19] In the
early 1860s, Dostoevsky had traveled to England, where
he observed both the Anglican and the Roman Catholic
churches. He was repulsed by the Anglican priests, who
seemed full of self interest, and impressed by the
Catholic priests for their dedication to the common
people. His reactions are detailed in his 1863 work
Winter Notes on Summer Impressions. Confirmed in his
Eastern convictions, he responded negatively to
Radstockism as a Western import. Dostoevsky had
direct contact with this movement through his lifelong
friendship with Julie Denisovna Zasetskaya, a

confirmed evangelical and the daughter of the well-known poet, Denis Davydov. In fact, she was one of the first to withdraw publicly from Orthodoxy because of her new convictions. Through her encouragement, Dostoevsky attended several meetings conducted by Radstock. As editor of *The Citizen*, he makes reference to the evangelicals in his regular column, "Diary of a Writer." In the March 1876 issue he gives an account and critique of the evangelical movement and of Radstock, but is chiefly critical of those who accept the English lord's teachings. He lays the blame for the "mirages" of the new teachings upon the people's separation from the real Russia and their "utter ignorance of their religion." He writes:

> ...the present success of Lord Radstock is based essentially, solely on "our segregation," our detachment from our soil, from the nation. It appears that at present we—i.e. the educated strata of our society—are an altogether alien little people, very little, quite insignificant, but a people who have their own customs and their own prejudices, which are taken for originality and as it now develops—with a desire for a religion of their own.[20]

Thus does Dostoevsky speak consistently from his aversion to Western culture and his love for Orthodoxy. Yet he is honest in his admission, "None the less, [Radstock] does produce extraordinary transformations and inspires in the hearts of his followers magnanimous sentiments."[21]

Dostoevsky also identified and rejected the work of Pashkov. Two accounts favorable to the latter appear in the *New Time*, May 11 and 13, 1880, in a period when negative reaction to Pashkov's activities was mounting. Dostoevsky sent a letter to the editor, A. S. Suvorin, in which he says:

...why do you praise Pashkov and why do you write that Pashkov performs a good deed in his preaching? And who is this [Orthodox] clergyman who some three days ago published with you a kind of defense of Pashkov? It is a miserable article—forgive me kindly for my frankness, but I am especially annoyed because all this appears in *New Time*—the newspaper which I love.[22]

While Dostoevsky did not incorporate these historic developments in his novels—*The Brothers Karamasov*, published in 1880, would have been the expected location—Tolstoy's *Anna Karenina*, finished in 1877, and considerably later, his *Resurrection*, did include allusions to the evangelical awakening. Tolstoy became acquainted with the movement through his friendship with Count Bobrinsky, a leading evangelical. Also, he received reports of first-hand encounters with Radstock by his aunt, A. A. Tolstaya. Tolstoy's closest associate, V. A. Chertkov, was a nephew of Pashkov, and reported positive feelings for him. Tolstoy, as well, was acquainted with the foreign preachers Dr. Baedeker and V. A. Ditman. Tolstoy once questioned his aunt, "Do you know Radstock? What impression did he make upon you?" He received this reply from Countess Tolstaya, written March 1876: "I have known Radstock quite well for the last three years, and I like him very much because of his extraordinary integrity and sincere love. He is fully devoted to a single cause and follows his path without turning to left or right...." The response goes on to critique Radstock: "He is a kind sectarian who does not understand everything and who in his naiveté fails to see in how many aspects he deviated from the gospel." She examines the possibility of instant salvation, which "is [Radstock's] weak point." Nevertheless, "his message resounded here like a bell, and he awakened many who before never thought of Christ and their salvation." Tolstoy, who had passed through much torment in his personal quest for salvation, responded sharply to what had been a balanced and generous critique. In April 1876, he answered, "How perfectly well you have described Radstock. Without having seen the original, one feels that he resembles a comical figure." Tolstoy goes on, "I was also happy with your opinion (if I understand you correctly) that instantaneous conversion does not occur at all or but rarely and that prior to it one has to undergo pains and tortures." Tolstoy admitted that he had to go through "suffering and agony" and considered the experience "the best of all my achievements," an achievement which he felt deserved to be rewarded.[23]

Anna Karenina was produced in serial form during the years 1875-1877 in the journal *The Russian Messenger*. In the story, which both recognizes and demeans the evangelical movement, Anna flirts with the ideas presented by the English missionary, Sir John, clearly an allusion to Lord Radstock. Her husband, Karenin, distraught when abandoned by Anna, turns to Sir John's teachings. Eventually, however, he realizes the shallowness of the evangelist's ideas and returns to his former ways.[24] Tolstoy, who consistently demonstrated a keen interest in moral and spiritual themes, weaves into the story his own conviction that the doctrine of justification by faith would lead to hypocrisy and unkindness. He was suspicious of the sincerity of the followers of Radstock, particularly those from among the aristocracy. His efforts were to slander rather than to understand the "new teaching," as he referred to the evangelical movement in his novel. Nevertheless, Tolstoy mirrors the concentration and the spiritual energies that thinkers in Russian society were expending during this period. His story exhibits the extent to which the movement had captured the attention of Pashkov's contemporaries.

Overt reaction to the evangelical movement was slow to develop. The awakening in St. Petersburg took place among the nobility, and "if there [was] freedom anywhere in Russia it [was] in the drawing room."[25] It was when the movement began to spread among the more reactive common classes that the authorities became more troubled. Nevertheless, the aristocratic evangelicals had friends in high places. Tsar Alexander II was Pashkov's friend, and such as A. E. Timashev, Minister of Internal Affairs, and General Trepov, Governor of St. Petersburg, were his relatives. Trepov was reported to have stated, "If Pashkov succeeds we [i.e., Russian society] are all saved." On several occasions, the governor had offered police protection for some of Pashkov's meetings, and newspaper advertisements of these meetings were tolerated.[26] By 1879, after five short years, the awakening had reached the zenith of its popularity. On one Sunday afternoon, 1,500 gathered for teaching at Pashkov's palace.

Yet there were signs of the coming reaction. Radstock was expelled in 1878, and, by imperial decree, public meetings of the evangelicals were prohibited. Excluded from this restraint were meetings in the home of the nobility, which were considered private venues. The Church publicly ordered Pashkov and his followers to abandon their error and return to the fold. In 1880 the turning point came. In that year, Pobedonostsev was appointed Chief Procurator of the Holy Synod and the Anti-Pashkov Society was formed in St. Petersburg.

K. P. Pobedonostsev was certainly unhappy with the evangelical development in the years leading up to 1880. During this time he was tutor to Alexander Alexandrovich, who was to become Tsar Alexander III. Pobedonostsev had joined with Prince Meschchersky and other conservatives in calling for the banning of the evangelical meetings and the expulsion of Radstock. In April 1880 his appointment came as Chief Procurator of the Holy Synod. Then in November he was made Minister of the Council of Ministries. Now he was in a position to intervene officially in the religious developments he found so objectionable. He had paid particular attention to the movement, had attended several of the evangelicals' meetings, and had prepared a file on their perceived offenses. On May 10, 1880 he reported in a private letter to the Tsar the findings of an extended meeting of a number of state ministers. Discussed were measures which might be taken against Pashkovism. This letter was shortly followed by an official memorandum to the Tsar. Professor Heier includes the full text of this document in his work, and excerpts are included here because of its dramatic depiction of the conflicting ideas which had emerged and its implications for the coming troubles for evangelicals. Pashkov is the central focus of this extended statement in which the life and activities of the movement are given, if pejoratively, in some detail.

> After the departure of Lord Radstock, who during his long stay here preached and held prayer meetings among the upper classes, which I regret to say, he did without being hindered, his follower, Mr. Pashkov, began to preach in the Russian language. He has now been preaching for two years [sic], and this he has done without permission, the Government laying no restraint upon him—in contravention of the law...which forbids the holding of meetings in this capital unknown to and without the approval of the authorities. [27]

The document describes Pashkov's preaching first among the upper classes, then increasingly among the common people, including "at the cabmen's lodgings" and "down to the lowest workman." His preaching was said to be "one-sided and narrow...extremely dangerous." His teaching, "i.e., love Christ, do not trouble yourself about good works, no good work will save you, Christ has already saved us once for all and nothing further is needed," would create among the masses "an indifference to sin, and...form an empty and fantastic faith and a love for Christ at once chimerical and presumptuous." Pashkov was accused of distributing tracts "translated from foreign languages, or written in the narrow spirit of the Radstock sect." He was also charged with having repudiated the Orthodox Church. Evidence of this was found in his preaching "without having received the blessing of the Church." He "avoids saying anything in reference to the Most Holy Virgin, Mother of God, or to the Saints—thus putting aside the doctrines of the Orthodox Church." In fact he "puts himself on a Protestant footing [and] orders his prayer meetings after the Protestant fashion." To the horror of Pobedonostsev, even the cabmen and workmen had become preachers!

Other examples are given of such unconstrained conduct among the nobility, all regrettably treated lightly by the authorities, according to Pobedonostsev. "The movement is far more important and dangerous than it may seem at first, and it is visibly gaining ground. These preachers are all of small capacities, of narrow-minded dispositions—but such men are the more dangerous founders of sects, for their stupidity makes them all the more persevering, obstinate, and concentrated...." Pobedonostsev gives as the basic reason for the success of this "schism" the "deep sense of religion" in the popular mind of the Russian people in which there "exists a belief in the mysterious sense of the Holy Scripture—this is the reason why all Russian sects have for foundation of their faith some one text of

Holy Scripture misunderstood or perverted." It was asserted that "The Church alone possesses the full, clear, catholic interpretation of the whole text in the sense of a catholic belief, and every one who separates himself from the Church, or sets himself up for a preacher, becomes a sectarian." Pobedonostsev concludes, "Therefore, before it is too late, it seems necessary without delay to put a stop to Pashkov's meetings…and to try to prevent the spreading the new sect, in reference to which the Church and the State, which have been undivided in Russia, cannot remain unconcerned." A five point prescription for action followed.

1.   Without further delay to recur to the measure foreseen in the 126th Clause of the Statute concerning the Prevention of Crimes, i.e., to forbid Pashkov's self-appointed prayer meetings and sermons.

2.   In consequence of the evident enthusiasm for Mr. Pashkov about the exclusive nature of his teaching, and his love of propaganda, it is necessary to send Mr. Pashkov away from Russia, if only for a time.

3.   To take active measures against similar meetings and sermons in St. Petersburg and other parts of Russia, if such should take place.

4.   To forbid Lord Radstock to visit Russia.

5.   In order to gratify the religious want which drew the people to Mr. Pashkov's meetings, it is necessary to call similar meetings and have prayers in the spirit of the Orthodox Church, with the assistance of the ablest and most zealous priests. This must be the care of the Church authorities in the capital as well as in the various dioceses.[28]

In the same month of May 1880, a special commission of high state officials submitted its unanimous opinion that Pashkov must be stopped. The Tsar, moved by these urgings, approved the measures recommended in the memorandum. On May 25, 1880, Pobedonostsev directed an order to the governor of St. Petersburg to implement these measures: "I, upon the ground of the Imperial order given to me, and having obtained the consent of the minister for the Home Department, ask your Honour to see that in future no prayer meetings be permitted to be held either at Mr. Pashkov's or at the abodes of his followers without being known and allowed by the authorities of St. Petersburg; and that no person shall preach God's Word in private lodgings and apartments." At the same time, the Tsar, no doubt with personal regret, ordered his friend Pashkov to leave St. Petersburg "for a time."[29]

Count Pashkov did leave for a brief stay to England but returned in a couple of months to his estate in the province of Moscow. At the nearby village of Kerkshin, where he had built a school and a hospital, he and his followers among the peasants held their meetings, and Pashkov continued on his work. In the spring of 1881, with a change of the authorities, he returned to the capital.

It was also in April 1880, at the very same time that fulminations by the authorities were being made against him, that Pashkov first openly responded to the accusations. The Anti-Pashkov Society's plan was to fight fire with fire. They distributed large amounts of printed materials, sent speakers into the cities and villages, and, where possible, engaged in debate with the Pashkovites. Priests and church leaders were encouraged to become students of the New Testament and to promote piety and good deeds. The flow of anti-Pashkovite material increased in Orthodox journals and Church papers. The evangelicals had hitherto maintained a low profile, determined not to answer their critics in print. A rare defense from Pashkov, however, surfaced in the May 10, 1880, issue of *Church Messenger*, an Orthodox organ edited by Archpriest John Yanishev, rector of the Theological Academy of St. Petersburg. In a letter to the editor, Pashkov detailed his beliefs and explained his motives for preaching.[30]

Pashkov's letter was received by Yanishev on April 9 but not printed until May 10, as subsequent letters were exchanged. Yanishev requested answers to pointed questions which, he believed, would clarify the main disagreement—the evangelicals' teaching on justification by faith versus the Church's doctrine of salvation by grace as dispensed by the priesthood and conditionally received through good deeds performed by the believer. Pashkov preferred that his original statement stand, and so it was printed. The exchange of correspondence was also printed, including Yanishev's questions and Pashkov's reply to them.

In Pashkov's original letter, he sets out the "essence" of his teaching. Prompted to write because of "distorted interpretations" of his teachings which recently have been repeated in the newspapers, he begins with a humble assessment.

> I don't have any theological knowledge (as you [the editor] allowed yourself to mention) and, therefore, being aware that I can easily make a mistake when interpreting these questions, I am not going to take part, in the future, in any polemics about them. I am willing in this case…to follow the commandment of the Lord: "Let not many of you become teachers knowing that we shall receive a stricter judgment" (James 3:1). I am satisfied with the only inspiration which I have from God: to call people to the Savior.[31]

Pashkov then proceeds, simply and with reference to a number of appropriate Scriptures, to detail his spiritual journey. He confesses to having lived "for forty years" in vanity, temptation, and in friendship with the world, supposing that "the Lord loves only such persons who were the first to love Him and earn His love for themselves." Then he speaks of his awakening: "The time came when the 'grace of God that brings salvation to all men' appeared to me (Titus 2:11), when the Lord decided to let me understand that the Christ, dying for the sins of the world, answered for my sins." Pashkov then moves through a series of Scriptures which amplify his understanding of this achievement of salvation through the grace of God.[32] The satisfaction which comes from finding himself in the assurance of the promises contained in these passages "overfills my heart with celestial joy." He then speaks of his work as a teacher of this good news. "The Lord has recruited me to His service—the service to which I have been consecrated for five years. It consists of witnessing to people about Him, about His limitless love which He lets me feel daily." Pashkov goes on to say, "I am repeating to everyone: 'Nor is there salvation in any other' (Acts 4:12). 'For no other foundation can anyone lay than that which is laid, which is Jesus Christ'" (1 Corinthians 3:11).

Then Pashkov answers the charge that he called the Church and the sacraments "the inventions of the Devil." This was the claim made by a certain Mr. Popov and carried in an earlier issue of the *Church Messenger*.[33] Pashkov states, "I said that any hope creeping into one's heart for the possibility of obtaining the kingdom of heaven by one's own deeds is no less than the invention of the Devil, making a person attach his hope to himself and not to the Lord." He then appeals to the Church's own position which, in the fifth point of its Anathema, excommunicates everyone "who does not accept the grace of redemption preached by the gospel as the only means of our justification before God." With further statements which emphasize that "true faith cannot help showing itself in deeds," and that Christian virtues are "nothing else but 'the fruit of the Holy Spirit'" (Galatians 5:22), Pashkov concludes, "Here is, in summary, the essence of what I am testifying before the people."

Then follow the texts of the several letters of the exchange between Yanishev and Pashkov. In one of them, Pashkov speaks of "the church" in such a way as to seem to point beyond the Church of Orthodoxy in Russia.

> The church of the living God is the pillar and ground of the truth (1 Timothy 3:15); it is the body of Christ (1 Corinthians 12:27), consisting of living members, i.e. believers in Christ redeemed by Him and loving Him, of members who have lived in Christ, and who are living now, or those whom the Lord will join to His body in the future. I cannot help recognizing its authority that, thanks to my Lord and Savior, I can consider myself belonging to His church.

Pashkov's confession appears to echo the conviction of Lord Radstock, who always maintained that he belonged to no other church but that of Christ. The Russian evangelicals did not counsel people to abandon the Orthodox Church during this period. Clearly though, they were committed to being "Christians only."

---

[1]   Edmund Heier, *Religious Schism in the Russian Aristocracy, 1860-1900: Radstockism and Pashkovism* (The Hague: Martinus Nijhoff, 1970), 55.

[2]   J. C. Pollock, *The Faith of the Russian Evangelicals* (New York: McGraw-Hill Book Company, 1964), 65.

[3] Heier, 83.

[4] L. N. Tolstoy, *Polnoe sobranie sochineny: Jubilejnoe izdanie, 1828-1928* (Moskva: ANSSR, 1928-58), LXX, 249, quoted by Heier, 84.

[5] L. N. Tolstoy, 306-7, quoted by Heier, 84.

[6] Sophie Lieven, daughter of Princess Lieven, wrote *Spiritual Revival in Russia* (Korntal, 1967) in which she described Madame Chertkova's prison work (cf. Brandenburg, 108).

[7] Hans Brandenburg, *The Meek and the Mighty: The Emergence of the Evangelical Movement in Russia* (New York: Oxford University Press, 1977), 106, 109.

[8] Edmund Heier states that N. S. Leskov, while lesser known, was one of a group of "religious, philosophical thinkers" such as Dostoevsky, Tolstoy, Leont'ev, Solov'ev, V. Rosanov and L. Shestov. Leskov's works include *No Way Out* (1864, in reaction to the reform movements of his day), *The Unbaptized Priest* (1872), *Cathedral Folks* (1872), *Details of Episcopal Life* (1878, cf. Heier 57). In 1876-77, he wrote *The Schism in High Society: Lord Radstock and His Followers*. His purpose was to counter the satirical attack of Prince Meschchersky against Radstock. In this work Leskov also became a critic of Radstock, a position which he later modified in his *Princely Slanders* (1884), published serially in the *News* (Heier, 69). "In seeking the rebirth of ideal Christianity, Leskov found himself in his later years favoring more and more a kind of Christianity which was neither national nor denominational" (Heier, 68).

[9] It is reported that sometime in the 1860s Pashkov donated the family palace in Moscow, situated next to the Kremlin, to the state. The Pashkov palace housed at first the library of the University of Moscow and subsequently became the core property of the Lenin State Public Library of the USSR, reputed to contain one of the world's largest collections.

[10] S. Glebov, "Polkovnik Pashkov," *Mission erskoe obozrenie* (Jan. 1904) III, 319-20, quoted by Heier, 116.

[11] Glebov, I, 84, III, 313, quoted by Heier, 114.

[12] The original members of the Society for the Encouragement of Spiritual and Ethical Reading were Radstock, Ostafieff (professor of history), Korff, Nicholson (manager of the British and Foreign Bible Society), Hall (a pastor), Gibson, Prince, Madame E. I. Chertkova, Madame M. G. Peuker, Princess Gagarin, and Pashkov. Pashkov was unanimously elected president. (Gregory L. Nichols, "Pashkovism: Nineteenth-Century Russian Piety," master's thesis, Wheaton College Graduate School, 1991,

48).

[13] Heier, 118.

[14] Pashkov published *Beloved Verses and Joyful Songs of Zion* in 1874 as relatively small collections, but in large editions (Brandenburg, 156).

[15] *The Russian Workman*, an eight-page monthly at first, was begun by M. G. Peuker before SESER agreed to fund its publication as a weekly. At Madame Peuker's sudden death in 1881, her daughter A. I. Peuker took over. It continued publication for two years after the closing of the SESER. The government organ, *The Official Messenger*, recommended *The Russian Workman* as one of the best publications for the people (Nichols, 49-52).

[16] Heier, 121.

[17] Heier, 8, quoting N. Berdyaev, *The Russian Idea* (London, 1947), 26-27.

[18] Heier, ix.

[19] Heier, 60, quoting Leskov.

[20] Nichols, 33-34, quoting F. M. Dostoevsky, *The Diary of a Writer* (New York: Octagon Books, 1973), 268.

[21] F. M. Dostoevsky, *Pis'ma v chetyrekh tomakh*, A. S. Dolinin, ed., (Moskva, 1959), vol. 1, 143, notes, 415, quoted by Heier, 62.

[22] L. N. Tolstoy, 266-67. This exchange is detailed in Heier, 84-6.

[23] See Heier, 84-6.

[24] *Anna Karenina*, Part V, Chapter 22; Part VII, Chapters 21-22; discussed by Heier, 86-91.

[25] Anatole Leroy-Beauliev, *The Empire of the Tsars and the Russians* vol. 3 (New York: G. P. Putnam's Sons, 1902), 471, quoted by Nichols, 43.

[26] Heier, 113.

[27] Heier quotes this document in its entirety, 126-129.

[28] Heier, 113.

[29] Heier, 130.

[30] The copy of the May 10, 1880 *Church Messenger*, No. 19, was located and supplied by the staff of the Saltykov-Shchedrin State Public Library and translated by Yuri Dobrokotov.

[31] Heier, 130.

[32] Hebrews 9:12; Romans 5:18; Hebrews 5:9; Colossians 1:21; Galatians 3:24; Matthew 9:13; Luke 19:10; Acts 10:43; Romans 5:15; Revelation 5:9; John 6:37; John 5:10-13; John 10:28; Hebrews 10:23; Luke 1:37.

[33] *Church Messenger*, No. 10.

9
oppression

Marc 1, 1881—Tsar Alexander II assassinated! Fearfully wounded by an initial blast from beneath his carriage, the Tsar made his way to examine a stricken coachman. A second bomb exploded, and the emperor was dead.

Dismay spread across Russia. The immediate result was the opposite of the revolutionaries' objectives: Alexander's murderers had intended to intimidate the next heir to the throne. Instead, the removal of the reformist Alexander II from the throne by violence opened the way for a resurgence of monarchism. His former tutor, Pobedonostsev, attended the young heir to the throne, Alexander III, who reacted with bitter opposition to any further reforms. In turn, his iron-fisted effort to shore up the Russian autocracy perpetuated the very conditions that led to the Bolshevik Revolution of 1917.

Alexander II had worked toward a more enlightened treatment of those who chose to move beyond the Orthodox Church. By decree on March 27, 1879, he had declared Baptist assemblies to be legal. Shortly before his death, Alexander had completed a provision that declared the right of freedom of conscience in Russia. Sophie Lieven, many years later, wrote about these days. Of her father, a Lutheran and master of ceremonies for the emperor, she said, "He often talked to [the emperor] about freedom of conscience in Russia. The emperor, who had great tolerance in religion, was preparing a corresponding law." Included was the permission for parents of mixed marriages to choose religion for their children. Approved by the senate, the pronouncement was to become law. Tragically, "the assassination ended that."[1]

Operating almost as a regent, Pobedonostsev supplied the vision of an empire strong because of absolutism and glorious because of its Church-sustained unity. In pursuit of this anachronism, Alexander III's determined decimation of the piety movement effectively removed Russia's one real hope—a new age of personal faith and peaceful harmony centered in New Testament Christianity. While cruelly suppressed and driven underground, the evangelical movement continued to spread, nourished in the classic tradition by the blood of its martyrs. The assault targeted first the leadership, then the apparatus, then the membership. Gradually, the oppression of the St. Petersburg Pashkovites merged with the persecution of the south-Russian Stundist peasants until a holocaust of abuse engulfed these and all sectarians. Bruised and bleeding, the movement suffered from the warping effects of the oppressive treatment.

The evangelical movement was, of course, an innocent bystander to the violence. Ironically, the evangelicals possessed the real answer to the anger and the inequity of the day.

> Though not possessing a definite social program, as for example, did the social revolutionaries, but merely advocating an evolutionary change with the Bible as their guidance, the Pashkovites were the only group of all social religious societies of the 1880s which could have initiated large-scale changes within the Russian Empire.[2]
>
> Proposals of love and brotherhood in Jesus' name

drew little attention, and the imperialists concluded that the evangelicals were dangerous to the state. The revolutionaries, on the other hand, identified the movement's aristocratic connections and concluded it was part of the problem. Caught in the middle, the evangelicals suffered accordingly.

Within an hour following the death of Alexander, Colonel Pashkov, who had recently returned to St. Petersburg, and his associates gathered to bow in prayer for the emperor's family and for the Russian people. Pashkov not only mourned the loss of a friend but also, no doubt, the passing of an era in which imperial sympathy had allowed some freedom for his preaching. Pashkov's last major project to spread the word of God in St. Petersburg was, in conjunction with the coronation of Alexander III, his free distribution of sixty-five wagon loads of Bibles to the people!

As detailed earlier, Pobedonostsev's efforts had succeeded during the last year of Alexander II's reign in enlisting the emperor's consent to restrain Pashkov's activities. The ascent to the throne by Alexander III secured unparalleled influence for the chief procurator. The violence that had taken his father terrified the young Tsar, and it now threatened his own safety. He was emotionally susceptible to suggestions for suppression and control. Pobedonostsev reminded him, as he had his father, of the failure to enforce the existing state law against assembly by dissenters. Alexander III, on March 3, 1883, reversed his father's 1879 decree, removing freedom of assembly for sectarians.

Konstantin Petrovich Pobedonostsev (1827-1907) was born of common ancestry. His grandfather was a rural priest, and his father, having risen among the intelligentsia, was a professor of literature at Moscow University. Afforded an education among children of aristocratic families, Pobedonostsev became enamored with the vision of a noble empire. By 1859, he was professor of civil law at Moscow University and by 1861 appointed royal tutor. His two passions were civil law and religion. In 1868, he published his *Handbook of Civil Law,* which became a standard text in Russia. In 1869, he translated *The Imitation of Christ* by Thomas a'Kempis and Heinrich Thiersch's *On Christian Family Life.* In 1880, he received appointment to the country's two most important posts, Chief Procurator of the Holy Synod and Religious Minister on the Council of Ministers— the reward for his intelligence, his religious fervor and his loyalty to the emperor. Pobedonostsev championed Orthodoxy on three fronts: he launched reforms to improve the training of the priests, moved to eliminate dissidents to the Church, and suppressed Protestant and Islamic influences pressing in on Russia's borders.[3] He was a man of prayer, sincerely convinced of the rightness of his position. He was, at the same time, arbitrary, devious, and ruthless in the pursuit of his objectives.[4] Largely because of him, the evangelicals suffered greatly. Count Witte, Prime Minister under Alexander III and Nicholas II, in his memoirs concerning Pobedonostsev, wrote, "...he strengthened the police regime in the Orthodox Church to the ultimate.... The history of Russia could have taken a different turn, in which case we would probably not have to experience the most base and senseless revolution and anarchy today."[5]

During the period 1882-1884, Pobedonostsev pursued his repression of the evangelicals. He ordered all bishops to report the progress of Pashkovism in their dioceses. In April of 1882, he directed a memorandum to the Minister of the Interior in which he reminded him of the May 1880 imperial decree that, significantly, remained unenforced. Pobedonostsev described "the increasing activity of Mr. Pashkov...[as a] remarkable boldness." Reports came "from all quarters, not only from the Most Holy Synod, but also from private individuals, information and bitter complaints." The memorandum gives a clear insight into both the temper of Pobedonostsev and the continuing expansion of the evangelical movement.

> This activity is particularly obnoxious, because it induces a fanatical tendency, and goes on in the spirit of Jesuitism and intolerance. As early as 1880 I was told that Mr. Pashkov and his agents persuaded the working people in the foundry to throw away their crucifixes, backing their persuasions by presents and help in need. When I personally reproached Mr. Pashkov with this, he did not deny it. Now, Mr. Pashkov, availing himself of his wealth, tries to lure to his doctrine the common and poor people; and as for his doctrine, I am sorry to say it advocates alienation from the Orthodox Church, creating enmity towards her, her institutions and ministers, with the flat denial of the worshipping of God's Mother and the adoration of the Holy Images....
>
> Mr. Pashkov's activity is not limited to the capital. His agents, recruited from among all classes of society, and not infrequently from ex-prisoners who pretend to be converted by him to the true faith, in the capacity of missionaries further his principles in the different parts of Russia where his teaching has already taken root.... All the above circumstances compel me to beg your Excellency to direct your attention to the activity of Mr. Pashkov, and to give orders to carry out the Imperial edict of 1880. I think that...Mr. Pashkov and Count Bobrinsky must be invited to leave for foreign parts.[6]

The leaders of the evangelical movement in St. Petersburg realized that conditions had altered radically as the result of the assassination, especially in the capital city. They did leave for distant, if not foreign, parts. Pashkov and Korff retreated to the region of the Volga in the spring of 1882. Bobrinsky, recently retired, moved to his estate in the province of Tula. Without their leaders and not permitted to meet openly, the evangelicals in St. Petersburg were quiescent for the next two years.

Activity continued, however, away from the capital. Pashkov and Korff became acquainted with the Stundists, the Baptists and the Molokans in the Ukraine and the Caucasus. Supplies of reading materials were made available to the southern evangelicals from the stores of the Society for the Encouragement of Spiritual and Ethical Reading. Pashkov's activities were wide-ranging: a workshop in Sevastopol for Stundists, land for a new colony of Baptists on the Don river, the employment of Molokans on his own estates, free land to peasants working in his copper mines south of the Urals. And wherever Pashkov went, he distributed free copies of the Scriptures.[7]

Pashkov rejoiced in the evidence of the spiritual awakening that he saw in the southern Russia revival. He found kinship among those who determined to reorder their lives on the foundation of the New Testament. A vision began to form in Pashkov's heart. Sophie Lieven recalled that Pashkov "particularly liked the idea of uniting into one brotherhood the believers of various names scattered all over Russia who were keeping the gospel."[8] All believers who attempted to practice a simple biblical faith must unite, he thought. After all, had not the Lord prayed that all who believed in him because of the apostolic message might be one? "May they be brought to complete unity to let the world know" that God had sent him to this earth.[9] The unification of the evangelicals, as they matured in the Word, was the logical next step. Thus motivated, Pashkov and Korff began in 1883 to plan for the gathering of Russian evangelicals in St. Petersburg in

April of the next year.

There were compelling reasons for the Pashkovites to take the lead in this forward step. They had made little effort, beyond a faithful and pietistic response, to shape their movement into a distinctive church structure and were thus the most open to accommodation. Their social concerns and spiritual convictions were compatible with those of the southern sects. They had the prestige of aristocratic leaders from the capital city and the strength of their publishing society. No doubt there was some anticipation that a united group could offer better protection against oppression. Indeed, one detractor saw the move as "the unification of all rationalistic sects so that they could move as a united force with greater success against the Orthodox faith."[10] Nor was the logic of these reasons lost on Pobedonostsev. Nothing could bring the conflict to a head more quickly than the proposed unity gathering.

Pashkov might be excused his miscalculation of Pobedonostsev's determination, considering his extended absence from the capital and the relative calm that had prevailed among the evangelicals there while the leaders were away. The decree of 1883 should have signaled, however, that the planned evangelical gathering in 1884 would be provocative.

Pashkov and Korff circulated widely their invitation to evangelical leaders throughout the empire. Representatives from the major sects—Molokans, Baptists, Stundists, Mennonites, and Dukhabors—as well as small splinter groups—traveled to St. Petersburg at Pashkov's expense and arrived in time for the April 1, 1884, beginning. To meet with them were the city's evangelicals, aristocrats, and commoners, as well as a number of foreign preachers, men from England, America, and Bulgaria. The ten-day meeting, to be conducted in the palaces of Pashkov, Korff, and Princess

Lieven, was unprecedented. Count Korff reported the observation of one Baptist, "The peasant sat next to the count and high society ladies served the common brethren."[11]

Yet beyond the good times, rich fellowship, and historic sense of the moment, disagreement began to surface on central issues. Baptism was essential for the Baptist but not for the Pashkovite. Access to the Lord's supper hinged on this obedience in the minds of a number of participants. Prospects for a working unity faded. Finally, the planned schedule set aside, they limited discussion to matters of morality and piety. In just twenty years of Russian evangelical activity, exclusive positions had hardened, and doctrinal unity proved elusive. Count Korff could conclude, nevertheless, that a unity of spirit had prevailed in spite of the lack of agreement. The future was promising.[12]

In the eyes of the religious authorities, however, no action could have been more inflammatory. Pashkov, whose presence in St. Petersburg was unwelcome, whose wide-ranging efforts in southern Russia had further stirred the sectarians, and whose disregard for the emperor's decree against unlawful assembly was inexcusable, had the audacity to convene this meeting under the very shadow of the imperial throne! Now was the time to root out for good the troublesome Pashkov and his cohorts, it was thought. The authorities broke up the meeting, dispatched its delegates, and, citing their provocation, exiled its leaders. One assessment of this startling action is given in a letter to Tolstoy by his assistant, V. G. Chertkov:

> Having returned to St. Petersburg, I became disgusted at the news that Pashkov and his co-religionist Korff are being expelled from Russia.... I am not upset at the government's behavior, which always applies the principle of

force, but I am disgusted that the Church, which considers itself the representative of Christ's teaching, approves such an act. I feel that this is the last drop for me. I do not share Pashkov's views, but at this moment, if I were asked to what religious affiliation I belong, I would say—to the Church of Christ without mentioning any of the recognized denominations.[13]

On May 24, the Society for the Encouragement of Spiritual and Ethical Reading was closed. Later, its stock of literature was confiscated. Homes where evangelical meetings took place were placed under police surveillance. Governors of the provinces and the bishops of their respective dioceses received instructions to identify and to curb the spread of Pashkovite activity. Pobedonostsev, the author of proper justice in Russia, brought secret accusations to the emperor against Pashkov and Korff. The emperor agreed to their guilt as arbitrarily defined by the chief procurator without opportunity for legal trial proceedings. "Chertkov maintains that in collecting his accusations against Pashkov, Pobedonostsev resorted to many arbitrary methods, defending these by saying that 'for the sake of a good cause, a lie is permitted.'"[14]

In June 1884, the Minister of Justice presented Pashkov and Korff with an ultimatum on behalf of the emperor: Sign a pledge to cease preaching, conducting Bible readings, and communicating with any sectarian, or suffer banishment from Russia. Of course, for these stalwarts, there was no option. Shortly, under police enforcement the Pashkov and Korff families departed for England and France, respectively. Pashkov's exile was permanent with the exception of one brief visit in 1887. Russia had lost two of its best men. Pobedonostsev had won. Or had he?

The evangelical movement was now a tide that

could not be repulsed, even by the removal of its two most influential leaders. Men in all stations of life continued to preach. Quantities of the society's publications escaped confiscation and were circulated. Reports came from virtually every diocese in Russia that confirmed the continuing spread of Pashkovism. One anonymous letter to Pobedonostsev in 1888 reported that since his exile Pashkov had supplied 6,000 religious books to the movement.[15] The papers, especially during the 1890s, increasingly reported trials of Pashkovites and various sectarians. Their "offenses" were such modest activities as distributing Bibles and tracts, conducting prayer meetings, and inviting others to Bible readings.

The emperor permitted Pashkov a brief return to Russia in 1887 since his son was gravely ill and Pashkov had some pressing business to attend to, namely the sale of his land to the peasants. Pobedonostsev, not consulted, became incensed when he learned that the emperor had permitted the visit. He directed a letter to the emperor.

> It is well known to your Imperial Highness what a pest was spread into the whole of Russia by the insane Pashkov.... Other hypocrites who respect no religion at all become agents of Pashkov...and spread all kinds of false rumors. One of these is that prominent people in the capitals, St. Petersburg and Moscow, including the Emperor and the Empress, have become Pashkovites or Stundists. The people see, indeed, that counts and princes and wealthy landowners who reside on their estates spread the teaching of Pashkov. In the capital itself one frequently meets gentlemen and ladies in highly placed positions, who although they do not belong to the dissenters, are in full sympathy with all sectarians and are ready to reject any measure

which is undertaken to curtail their propaganda.

Since [their banishment]...Pashkov and Korff...not only did not stop their propaganda, but Pashkov especially, continued it through his agents. Considering his enormous wealth and his many estates in various provinces, he has at his disposal considerable means to finance such propaganda. Since the managers on his estates are ardent sectarians and since he employs a multitude of workers in his factories and plants it becomes clear what kind of propaganda weapons he is operating....[16]

The emperor sent a terse reply in which he corrected several of Pobedonostsev's assumptions but agreed to "expedite [Pashkov's] departure." According to one report, the Tsar said to Pashkov, "I hear you have resumed your old practices." Pashkov admitted reading the Bible and praying with some of his own friends. "Which," the Tsar replied, "you know I will not permit.... Now go and never set foot upon Russian soil again."[17]

The tone of Pobedonostsev's letter to the emperor reflected his frustration, and the emperor's reply, while acceding to Pobedonostsev's concerns, was not as compliant to his demands as the chief procurator might have hoped. As a consequence, from the late 1880s Pobedonostsev's persecution of the evangelicals became more focused, organized and violent. He pushed for the strictest enforcement of Paragraph 187 of the penal code: "For enticing Orthodox Christians into any other confession, the guilty person is condemned to the loss of all particular personal rights, and those adhering to his status, and to exile in Siberia or dispatch to the convict corrective labor brigade."[18] The convicted faced loss of position, loss of property, loss of children, loss of freedom, and exile. The clear message was, "Either return to Orthodoxy or suffer." Countless numbers chose to suffer. Sophie Lieven recounted of those days, "Prison and exile...[were] the usual fate[s] awaiting believers."[19]

Even in this process Pobedonostsev met reverses. The trials exposed the sincerity and the courage of the accused, and to many Russians they appeared as martyrs rather than criminals. Those exiled preached the word of God where they were sent and planted the faith in remote corners of the land. Word of the brutal treatment of believers spread around the world, outraging many. Even some within the Church were repulsed by the strong-arm tactics being used. "As early as 1887, the Russian Minister of Justice, Count von Pahlen, himself a follower of Radstock, likened the persecution of Russian sectarians to that of the Inquisition."[20]

There was some unevenness in the persecution, however, in the capital, where many of the aristocracy, in positions of influence, were themselves either evangelical believers or estranged from the Church. Following Pashkov's exile, meetings of the evangelicals shifted from his home to the palace of Princess Lieven at 43 Great Morskaya, site of the aborted dinner. Her daughter, Sophie, described the reaction.

> Soon after [the moving of the meetings], the general adjutant of the emperor came to my mother. He came with the commission to tell her that His Royal Majesty wished the meetings in her house to be stopped. My mother, who was always caring about the souls of her neighbors, began at first to talk to the general about his soul and about the need to be reconciled with God.... Then answering his commission, she said, "Ask His Royal Majesty whom I must obey more, God or the emperor?" There was no answer to this

unique and quite brave question. The meetings continued.... It was conveyed to my mother later on that the emperor said, "She is a widow. Leave her in peace." Some years ago, I heard from one person, competent in this issue, that there was a plan to exile both my mother and Elizaveta Ivanovna Chertkova. It seems that Alexander III, though he did not share the views of the evangelical believers, as a God-fearing person, did not want to do any harm to widows. That is why he did not allow this action. Thus, the meetings carried on for many more years in our house. Regarding the defenseless and human weakness of these two widows, the Lord had shown his strength.[21]

Pobedonostsev supported absolutism, and he acted autocratically in the name of the emperor, often without divulging to the emperor his moves. This was his strategy when he dealt with the Baltic Lutherans. In the midst of the forced Russification of the Baltic states, Pobedonostsev suppressed severely the Lutherans whose "foreign" presence he found so objectionable. "It seems Alexander III had little knowledge of the extent of violence poured on the Lutherans in the Baltic."[22]

The second way by which Pobedonostsev sought to achieve his objectives was by mounting every possible pressure upon his ministerial colleagues to gain his ends. His influence with the emperor assured a measure of success. Pobedonostsev's elevated vision of the Church and the empire was the theme of his speech in Kiev in 1888—the occasion of the 900th anniversary of Prince Vladimir's introduction of Christianity to Russia.

It is terrible to think what would have become of us, had it not been for this Church. She alone, she alone helped us to remain Russians.... The Russian house of God is the home of the Russian man. It is here that our strength is rooted, here we find the secret treasure-store of our destiny.... If anyone strays from her, with God's help he will return to his home and his mother.... We have become great beneath this banner of absolute power and autocracy; we still stand beneath this banner, here we see the future's guarantee of truth, order and the country's well-being.[23]

Pobedonostsev gave this speech of triumphant loyalty with the troubling knowledge, however, that almost every village in the surrounding region was 'infected' with Stundism. "It is not surprising that 1888 was to be the beginning of the systematic extermination of Stundism."[24] Two conferences were held in Moscow in 1891. Their resolutions, made public in May 1893, were declared to be the "law against the Stundists" in July 1894. The severity of these proscriptions is frightening.

- The children of the Stundists are to be taken from their parents and put in the charge of relatives who belong to the Orthodox Church; if this is impossible, then they are to be put in the care of the local clergy.

- Henceforth it is forbidden for the Stundists to hold services or to establish schools.

- The Stundists' passports and identity documents are to carry a reference to their adherence to a sect. Any employer who takes a Stundist into service is subject to high fines.

- The names of the members of this sect are to be sent to the Minister for Roads and Railways, who will have them posted in railway offices, so that they cannot find employment there.

- A Stundist is forbidden to employ an Orthodox. Infringements are to be punished by exile to the Caucasus for up to five years.

- Stundists are forbidden to buy or lease land. Any Stundist who is discovered reading the Bible or praying with others is to be imprisoned and immediately sent to Siberia by administrative means [without trial]; all preachers are to be sentenced to forced labor in the mines there.

- Stundists are to be buried away from consecrated ground; it is forbidden to hold a funeral service for them.

- All sectarians are forbidden to leave their places of residence. They are to be declared legally incapable of transacting financial and trading business.

- Preachers and authors of religious writings are to be sentenced to 8-16 month's imprisonment, for a second offense to 32-48 months' imprisonment in a fortress, on a third occasion to exile.[25]

Not only did the Stundists suffer at the hand of the state, local prejudice and personal intolerance found excuses to heap indignities upon the believers as well. Hermann Dalton, Reformed Church pastor in St. Petersburg, in his 1906 memoirs, reflected on his personal exposure to the persecuted Stundists.

During my travels in the Caucasus I saw the wretched exiles.... Like criminals they were dragged off with their families...to the borders of the empire where wild Kurdish tribes lived.... Into these remote regions they came by the hundreds, not to be settled but simply banished there and left to their own devices, these poor wretched Stundists whose only crime is to believe the holy gospel and to want to live by it.... As these people slowly languish and die in terrible misery in the south of the empire, so too we see more of those persecuted for their faith following the long, hard path to Siberia....[26]

The Pashkovites, who were reported to have forty houses of prayer throughout the capital and, in the city at least, were functioning "without prohibition," began now to experience full-scale oppression as pressure increased to treat all sectarians in the same severe way.[27] The Commission of the Third All-Russian Missionary Congress, conducted in 1896 in Moscow, studied the similarities between Stundism and Pashkovism. One of the witnesses, V. M. Skvortsov, reported to the Commission that he had found in the archives of a governor-general in south Russia documents which contained correspondence between Pashkov and leaders of the Stundists. This correspondence had begun very early in the beginning of Pashkovism and continued "until now."[28] The conclusion reached was that both were guilty of similar teachings and unlawful activity. Both must "fall under the action of the decision of the Council of Ministers of September 1894, approved by the emperor, about recognizing this sect as particularly harmful, and forbidding any public prayer meetings of its followers. There must be one name, Stunda, in the nomenclature of sects for all its factions."[29]

The oppressive treatment of the Russian evangelicals did seriously impact their development. Systematically suppressed, they were denied their rightful place in the center stage of Russian history. Confusion set in as the Stundists gravitated to the

Baptists. The Pashkovites, their leadership scattered and their membership stumbling, ultimately disappeared as a distinct movement.

The Baptists, drawing strength from the world Baptist movement, gained during the difficult last two decades of the century. Following the failed unity initiative in St. Petersburg in 1884, the Baptist delegates reconvened several weeks later in the Ukrainian village of Novo-Vasil'enka, where they formed the Russian Baptist Union. John Weiler was elected president. When he was forced to escape into Romania, he was succeeded by Dei Mazaev, who give solid leadership up until the time of the Revolution.[30] The Stundists chose to follow either *mladostundism*, the "spiritual" Stundists, or *starostundism*, Stundists who practiced baptism. A number of the latter chose to move into the Baptist fellowship. For these, the vision of a nondenominational expression of Christianity gradually faded.

The Pashkovites were most open and ecumenically minded in their determination to be Christians without denominational ties. Their initial impulse was simply to restore the spirit and piety of New Testament Christianity. In the beginning they had no intention either to leave the Church or to criticize it. However, the trappings of Orthodoxy—the adoration of Mary, prayers to the saints and for the dead, devotion for icons and relics, and the doctrine of salvation by works—became less and less acceptable as biblical knowledge grew. Their clearing vision was coupled with their increasing rejection by the Church. Still there was little inclination to form an official church as such. A natural progression was experienced, nevertheless. To their "calling out" (evangelistic) meetings, they added "praying" meetings and then Sunday "worship" meetings. Baptism was advocated, but its timing was left to the individual as each felt called by the Scriptures and the Spirit to comply. Participation in the Lord's

supper was also desired but only when the individual
felt ready for this step.[31] Neither of the observances were
felt to have the inherent power of Orthodox sacraments.
Nor did they serve simply as the door to and seal of
membership in a local church, as in the tradition of the
Baptist Church. Clearly, both observances provided
direct spiritual linkage with the Savior. A cleavage began
to develop among the Pashkovites, however, over the
imperatives of baptism, the Lord Supper, and a more
structured fellowship. Pashkov's return in 1887 was
intended in part to deal privately with the
disagreements between the older group, under the
influence of the widows Madame Chertka, Countess
Gagarina, and Princess Lieven, who favored the more
open stance advocated by Radstock and Pashkov, and
a younger group meeting elsewhere in the city who
sensed the need for a clear vision as a church.

The casual structure of the Pashkovites,
compounded by the loss of their able leaders, left them
especially vulnerable to the pressures of persecution.
The failure to find male replacements for Pashkov and
Korff among the aristocracy indicates that the
movement was fading among the upper classes. The
leaders drawn from lower levels of society brought with
them, in the minds of some, a narrowing of the vision.
In the face of mounting opposition, some became
dormant, some returned to the Church, and some
moved to the Stundists or to the Baptists. A number were
attracted to the more structured option offered by the
young engineer, I. S. Prokhanov, and these became the
core group of the Evangelical Christians of the 20th
century.

As Pashkov approached death in Rome in 1902,
did he ponder, "Was it all in vain?" Or did he go to his
reward confident in his Lord's ability to "keep that
which [he] had committed unto him until that day"?
Did he die in hope that the seed planted in the

nineteenth century would some day produce a stalk, a head, a hundredfold harvest? V. G. Chertkov, Tolstoy's disciple and assistant, reflected on his uncle's passing.

> Having been in close relation with the family of Vasili Alexandrovich, I was well acquainted not only with his public activities but also with him personally in his private life. And I can say without exaggeration that I have never met a person purer and kinder, more conscientious, more magnanimous, more delicate, more generous and nobler in the full meaning of these words, than Pashkov."[32]

In the Pashkov palace in Moscow, given by the colonel to the state in the 1860s and now the location of the Russian state public library, claimed by some to be the world's largest, there is presently no record preserved of Vasili A. Pashkov, one of Russia's truly great benefactors and spiritual giants. Perhaps both his memory and his vision will be restored to bless Russians everywhere as the new millennium opens.

---

[1] Sophie Lieven, *Spiritual Revival in Russia* (Korntal, 1967), 19.

[2] Edmund Heier, *Religious Schism in the Russian Aristocracy, 1860-1900: Radstockism and Pashkovism* (The Hague: Martinus Nijhoff, 1970), 136.

[3] Robert Byrnes, *Pobedonostsev, His Life and Thought* (Bloomington: Indiana State University Press, 1968), 174-76, quoted in Gregory L. Nichols, "Pashkovism: Nineteenth Century Russian Piety" (master's thesis, Wheaton College Graduate School, 1991).

[4] Hans Brandenburg, *The Meek and the Mighty: The Emergence of the Evangelical Movement in Russia* (New York: Oxford University Press, 1977), 115.

[5] Brandenburg, 115.

[6] W. T. Stead, *Truth About Russia* (London, 1888), 376-78; quoted by Heier, 132-33.

[7] Heier, 134.

[8] Lieven, 20.

[9] John 17:21, 23.

[10] G. Terletsky, "*Seckta pashkotsev*," *Pravoslavnoe obozrenie* (Jan. 1890, II 1-58), 52, quoted by Heier, 135.

[11] V. Pavlov, "*Vospominanija ssl'nago*," *Materialy k istorii I izucheniju russkago sektautstva iraskola*, V. Bronch-Bruevich, ed. (St. Petersburg, 1908), I, 4, quoted by Heier, 137.

[12] M. M. Korff, Am Zarenhof, *Erinnerungen aus der Geistlichen Erweckungsbewegung in Russland von 1874-1884*, Tr. M. von Kroeker (Wernigerode am Harz, 1927), 60, quoted by Heier, 137.

[13] L. N. Tolstoy, *Polnoe sobranie sochineny: Jubilejnoe izdanie, 1828-1928* (Moskva: ANSSR, 1928-58), quoted by Heier, 94.

[14] Chertkov, "V. A. Pashkov [*Nekrolog*]," *Svobodnoe slovo* (1902, March), No. 3, 23, quoted by Heier, 138.

[15] Heier, 140.

[16] K. P. Pobedonostsev, *Pis'ma Pobedonostseva k Aleksandru III*, M. N. Pokrovsky, ed., 2 vols. (Moskva, 1925), II, 158-60, quoted by Heier, 142.

[17] Robert Sloan Latimer, *Dr. Baedeker in Russia and His Apostolic Work* (London: Morgan and Scott, 1907), 35.

[18] Brandenburg, 122.

[19] Lieven, 20.

[20] Heier, 144.

[21] Lieven, 21.

[22] Nichols, 65.

[23] Brandenburg, 120-23

[24] Brandenburg, 123.

[25] Brandenburg, 123-24.

[26] Dalton, *Der russische Stundismus*, 50-51; quoted by Brandenburg, 126.

[27] The report of F. N. Ornatsky, editor of the *Spiritual Herald* of the St. Petersburg Eparchy, one of four who reported to the All-Russian Missionary Congress. See Ornatsky, "*Pashkovshchina i ishtundism*," *Missionerskoe obozrenie* (Sept.-Oct. 1897), II, No. 1, 800-6, quoted by Heier, 145.

[28] "Pashkovism," 7.

[29] "Pashkovism," 8.

[30] Walter Sawatsky, *Soviet Evangelicals since World War II* (Scottsdale, PA: Herald Press, 1981), 44.

[31] "The Novice's Story," *Theological Herald*, trans. Yuri Dobrokhotov (Moscow Theological Academy, Vol. 2, March 1893), 522-33.

[32] Chertkov, 22, quoted by Heier, 110.

10
The Evangelical Christians

The opening years of the twentieth century were portentous for Russia. The flash point was near, but the imperial order moved doggedly toward its tragic conclusion. Tsar Nicholas II was uncomfortable as an autocrat yet resistant to reducing his absolute power. Russia was now the world's fifth largest industrial power, but her workers lived and labored in appalling conditions. Unions were illegal; there was no right to strike; and the work day was reduced to a "mere" eleven-and-a-half hours only in 1897. With emancipation nearly a half century old, the peasant farmers—ninety percent of all Russians—were still mired in poor land distribution, poor production practices, and recurring famine. Russia's stinging defeat in the Russo-Japanese War of 1904-1905 sent a signal to Russian leaders: the Russian bear, potentially powerful but ponderously inept, had not graduated to the advancements of the new century as had other nations.

The forces of liberation fed on massive and growing discontent. The revolt of 1905 was largely a peasants' rebellion, engulfing much of rural Russia. Armed conflict took place also in the major cities, beginning in St. Petersburg on "Bloody Sunday," January 9, when soldiers opened fire on unarmed citizens. The "Social Revolutionaries" who supported the nationwide protests were carefully watched by the more sinister Social Democrats and the Bolsheviks they harbored. The army, which remained loyal to the Tsar, suppressed the 1905 uprisings, which were largely spontaneous and uncoordinated. One result, however, was the creation of the state Duma, or parliament, which offered some hope of a future democracy.[1]

In the meantime, the Bible-born movement had been dealt a cruel blow and was incapable of providing leaven for a nation poised on the brink of disaster. In the midst of this turmoil, little note was paid to Pashkov's death in 1902 in far-off Rome. Truly an admirable Russian, Pashkov represented the best of Russia's aristocracy. His passing foreshadowed the end of the nobility, a class that generally had taken much and given little to Russia.

Another event occurred in 1902 that, while of minor import on the broader stage, had special significance. It was the publication of a hymnbook entitled *Gusli* ("Harp," or "Psaltery") by Ivan S. Prokhanov. Twenty thousand copies were printed and immediately distributed among Evangelicals across Russia. Remarkably, this religious work, published by a dissenter for use by "sectarians," was manufactured by the Director of the Printing Bureau of the Ministry of the Interior! Those pursuing the persecution of dissenters across the nation were taken aback when they came upon these hymnbooks bearing the stamp of the government's printer. Clearly, a mistake had been made, and they must confiscate those books! But they had all been distributed. The Evangelicals, for years driven underground, had worshipped with the help of handwritten hymnals. They now had a precious collection in print. Included were compositions inspired by the Evangelicals' fresh vision of the faith and forged by their trials. The gifted Prokhanov had composed many of the selections. His initiative in securing the printing, reflecting boldness and a genius for getting things done, was a foretaste of his future leadership. *Gusli* was a symbol of a movement that was vitally alive and growing.

The Evangelical Christians, direct descendants of the Pashkovites, kept before them the vision of a Christians-only movement in Russia in the early years of the new century. They pursued the goal of the unity of all believers on the basis of biblical authority. They attempted to give congregational expression to the simple faith of the earlier "believers." They worked not only for a spiritual reformation but also for the social regeneration of the Russian people. Now badly outdistanced by the growing, violent revolution, the Evangelical's efforts were, nevertheless, revolutionary for their age. They advanced egalitarianism in a class-stricken society. They exchanged pacifism and love for coercion and abuse. They championed a religion of faith and freedom in contrast to the Church's insistence on works and ecclesiastical monopoly. While the coming revolution would establish atheism as the state religion, denigrating faith in God as an "opiate of the people," the Evangelicals remained faithful even to death. They bequeathed such a spiritual heritage to Russia that a hundred years later the people could confidently affirm, "The real revolution is coming!"

Into the vacuum created by the exile of such leaders as Pashkov, Bobrinksy, and others moved Ivan Stephanovitch Prokhanov, a natural leader who, almost single-handedly, led the Evangelical Christians to remarkable heights during the first quarter of the twentieth century.

Prokhanov arrived in St. Petersburg in 1888 to pursue an education in engineering at the imperial Institute of Technology. He was nineteen years of age, a believer, and a dissenter. He soon became deeply immersed in the activities of the Evangelicals. Prokhanov's parents were of Molokan stock who, in 1862 because of persecution, had fled from their home in Saratov province. They settled in the city of Vladikavkas in the Caucasus province of which Tiflis (Tbilisi) was capital. Ivan, born April 17, 1869, was a precocious child. As a youth he read extensively in the classics of Russian literature and developed abilities in composition and poetry. In his youth he was surrounded by the spiritual influences of his family and a community of "believers" that existed in Vladikavkas.[2] Exposed to rationalism and nihilism in his high school years, Ivan succumbed to a severe depression and contemplated suicide. Perceptively, his father had removed from the house a rifle which Ivan had been eyeing and left in its place a note reading, "Do you love Jesus Christ?" This experience led to his conviction and baptism in the River Terek in November 1886. As a teenager, Prokhanov became active in the life of the local congregation, teaching children and beginning to preach.

Prokhanov set two goals for his life: to spread the Word of God and to bring relief to his beloved Russia. He developed the habit of planning for each day, each month, each year, and each phase of a predetermined program for his life. As a result, he became highly productive, his genius for organization well-matched by his boundless energy. He decided upon a career in engineering so that he might, like the apostle Paul, be self-supporting in his ministries. He chose to apply to the Technological Institute in St. Petersburg, where entrance was gained by only one out of every five applicants. He spent 1887-1888 preparing for the entrance exam and scored among the top five of some two hundred who were admitted.

During his student years in St. Petersburg, Prokhanov engaged in the closeted meetings of the Evangelicals, often conducted in the mansion of Princess Lieven. Here he met J. B. Kargel, who reflected the more open spirit of Pashkov. He had contact, as well, with William Fetler, who was acknowledged as the leader of the Russian Baptists. In St. Petersburg, Prokhanov also came under the influence of the religious philosopher, Vladimir Solov'ev, who stressed the importance of the unity of all believers. Secret meetings of the Evangelicals were conducted throughout the city with changes of location for each meeting. People arrived and departed singly. Raids were frequent; arrested leaders would regularly be exiled for eight to thirteen years. Prokhanov participated and preached often. As a student, he began a growing correspondence with believers across the country and sought intervention for the many injustices they suffered. There were secret believers in all departments of the government who were willing to help, as well as sympathizers in the senate, the council, and among the lawyers.

In the spring of 1889, Prokhanov determined to circulate a periodical to lend encouragement to the harried believers. While home for a summer visit, he and his brother constructed a hectograph.[3] His publication *Beseda* ("Conversation," or "Talking") was titled as unobtrusively as possible. In the fall, Prokhanov took his hectograph back to St. Petersburg and continued to publish from his small room. His lodgings were with a family who were believers and sympathetic to his activity. The writers used pseudonyms: Prokhanov's was "Zacchaeus," because of his large stature! Copies were posted—by registered mail, to avoid the censors—to the main Evangelical congregations, their preachers, and even to those in exile, with resulting great encouragement.

The students at the Technological Institute were known for their political activity. Prokhanov agreed with their ultimate aim, the improvement of the Russian people through social reform, but he insisted that this could be achieved only by means of spiritual regeneration.

> For me the teaching of Jesus Christ was the only real way to the spiritual regeneration of an individual, of society, of nations and the whole of humanity. In debates with my fellow students of the political group I always argued that, although extreme political and social reforms were necessary for the Russian people and must be obtained, the regeneration of the spiritual life was still more necessary. I maintained that no political reform could be put into practical effect if the people remained in the darkness of the Orthodox Church with its fetishism. No social or political reforms could prove successful unless a moral and spiritual reform in the people themselves was first realized.[4]

Prokhanov completed his studies in 1893 and received his diploma in August of that year. Upon his graduation, Prokhanov and a friend, en route to their homes in the Caucasus, paid a special visit to Leo Tolstoy at his estate, Yasnaia Poliana, near Tula. Walking with Tolstoy, they said, "We are aiming at being disciples of Christ, and we would like to have a talk with you about Christ." Tolstoy gave them his new work to read, *The Kingdom of God Is within You,* while he went into the forest to pick mushrooms. Later, over a mushroom meal, they conversed on their respective understandings of Christianity, neither giving way to the other. Prokhanov's assessment of their meeting is contained in his autobiography:

After the conversation with Tolstoy, I became more firmly convinced that the salvation of the world is in the simple Gospel, not in a part of the Gospel, but in the whole Gospel.... [T]he doctrine of Tolstoy...is simply a moral teaching, which transforms Christ's grace into the Mosaic law or the Stoic principle, because it brings men to an inaccessible mountain and without imparting to them any power says: "Climb up." Of course, they cannot climb up.... Of course, there can be no other result than the consciousness of utter hopelessness and despair.[5]

Prokhanov first took employment with the wealthy socialist Nepluev as assistant director of his sugar factory in Chernigov province. His activities soon marked him as a Stundist. His differences with Nepluev were such that he left in February 1894 to work with a shipbuilding firm at Colpino, near St. Petersburg. Soon, filled with youthful optimism, Prokhanov and several friends moved to the Crimea and established a communal enterprise on an estate near Simferopal.

They called their community "Vertograd"—the "Ideal City,"—and "Vineyard", for both physical and spiritual reasons. An idyllic experience was cut short, however, when it was learned that Prokhanov's father had been exiled for distributing religious literature. Prokhanov traveled to Vladikavkas to assist his mother, then on to St. Petersburg to intervene on behalf of his father. On September 3, 1894, the anti-Stundist law was passed, and persecution intensified. Vertograd was discontinued and the estate sold. Prokhanov's friends prevailed upon him to leave Russia, for he was under threat of arrest. It was determined that *Beseda* would continue and be published in Stockholm and Prokhanov would seek assistance for the Evangelical movement from abroad. It was January 1895.

In danger of detection and arrest at any moment, Prokhanov was assisted by a Finnish pastor in his flight through Finland, which was Russian territory at the time. Eventually, he was hidden in "the castle of Baron H., a sincere Christian brother, sympathizing with all sufferers for Christ's sake."[6] Here he stayed for ten weeks, waiting for the ice to clear from the port of Abo, from which he would sail to the West. For the next three-and-a-half years, until late in 1898, Prokhanov visited in England, Berlin, and Paris. In each place he enrolled in colleges and universities and pursued theological studies. He also sought aid for Russian believers in their distress and maintained extensive correspondence with them. He was greatly impressed with the freedom and openness he experienced in Protestant lands. He observed, "The more I studied other denominations, the more I became faithful to my own Russian Evangelical conception of Christianity, which I regarded at the time and still believe to be the form nearest to the primitive Christianity of the Apostles."[7]

In September 1898, Prokhanov was requested to proceed from Paris to Cyprus to assist a community of some 1,150 Dukhobors who were emigrating from Russia to Canada because of the persecution. These refugees were being held in a camp because of an epidemic of dysentery. Prokhanov helped to organize their recovery efforts and served the authorities as a translator. He was encouraged to accompany the Dukhobors to Canada, but the call to return to Russia was strong. He arrived in Constantinople without a passport and was arrested. Passed from one jurisdiction to another under police guard, he finally arrived at Vladikavkas, where he regained his freedom. He then set out to find his exiled father in Armenia. After a reunion of five days, Prokhanov returned to his work in Russia. In Riga he gained employment as an assistant manager of a railway and taught as an assistant professor at the Polytechnical Institute. During this period he became engaged to Anne Ivanovna Kazakova of Tiflis and married her on August 31, 1901. In the same year, by orders of the Minister of the Interior, he was removed from his teaching post because of his "Stundist" involvement. Soon, however, he was able to secure a position with the Westinghouse Company, located in St. Petersburg, supplying air brakes to the Russian train system. With his papers as an employee of this company, he was able to move freely around the country and to travel overseas. In danger of arrest because of his initiative with the *Gusli* publication, Prokhanov, fortunately, was sent to America to study engineering methods and accomplishments in that country. He left Russia for a time in April of 1902.

Continued agitation by the liberation movement in Russia was having its effect. The people spoke of a "coming spring" in which social liberties would surely arrive. As noted before, under the pressure of the growing troubles, Nicholas II, on February 26, 1903, issued a special manifesto in which the principle of freedom of confession of faith would be extended to all denominations and religions. However, all the old laws concerning religious life continued on the books. These laws were pressed in many parts of Russia, unaffected by the manifesto.[8]

The Evangelicals, with Prokhanov's bold initiatives, helped nudge the state into honoring the principles of freedom of conscience espoused in its decrees and manifestos. The new Minister of the Interior, Prince Sviatopolk-Mirsky, in his pursuit of a course of "confidence toward the people," announced that he wanted to receive information concerning all religious societies, denominations, and churches. Prokhanov responded by writing "The Report to the Ministry of the Interior Concerning the Legal Condition of Evangelical Christians, Baptists and Others in Russia." The report documented the persecutions, imprisonments and exiles that the Evangelicals had experienced and gave suggestions for the necessary changes in the religious laws. These recommendations were examined by the Manifesto Commission and were contained largely in the government's Act of Toleration, published on April 17, 1905. The Act, entitled "On the Strengthening of Religious Tolerance," gave the right of separation from the established Church.[9] Sophie Lieven remembered those days.

> In April 1905 in the morning of the Day of Lights of Christ's Resurrection [Easter] in the house, number 43 Morskaya, there was a meeting and many people were present there. Brother Ordintsov read the tsar's decree.... All knelt and praised God for this gift.[10]

This was the year of the peasants' revolts and the disastrous war with the Japanese. Subsequently, under the pressure of these events, and at the advice of the president of the Council of Ministers, S. U. Witte, the Tsar issued the Manifesto of October 17, 1905. In the words of Prokhanov, "In this manifesto, toleration was changed to freedom of conscience and the autocracy was changed into a parliamentary form of government. Freedom of press, of meetings, organization of societies and freedom of political activities was proclaimed."[11]

One would have had to suffer the indignities and deprivations of the long reign of terror to appreciate fully the joy and relief that this proclamation brought the evangelistic groups in Russia! Pobedonostsev, unable to cope with the new Russia, resigned all his posts.[12] Following the manifesto, some of those in exile were released. Many were not, however. Prokhanov and Dolgopolov, an elder of the St. Petersburg Evangelical

Church, personally delivered a petition to Prime Minister Witte with the result that all who were imprisoned or exiled for religious reasons were released. "Large and immediate use was made of the new liberty. Meetings were held everywhere—crowded with hearers who seemed as though they never could hear enough of the Word.... Many hidden companies of believers came to light and it became evident that the number of...disciples was far larger than had been supposed."[13]

The years leading up to the Great War, 1914-1918, were full and exciting for the Russian Evangelical Christians. While religious privileges, in practice, were often less than promised, the freedom to preach and develop congregations without the fear of the secret police was received with deep gratitude. Further clarification to the October 17, 1905, manifesto was given a year later, in the October 17, 1906, decree "On the Order and Formation and Action...for Communities." This decree gave a basis for the legalization of the Evangelical and Baptist churches. To register a church, an application bearing fifty signatures was to report the election of a presbyter-teacher acceptable to the government. The first Evangelical Christian church to be registered was in St. Petersburg in 1908.[14] The congregation was organized, activities divided, a constitution established, and a council elected. Prokhanov was named president of the council, a post he held for twenty years, until 1928.[15]

Delegations of Evangelical Christians and Baptists met in 1907 to discuss the 1906 decree and to make suggestions for its improvement. Later, Prokhanov composed a book *Law and Religion*, into which he gathered the various laws that had been passed, along with comments and interpretations. This work proved invaluable to church leaders who had to deal with provincial authorities. Even the officials found the handbook to be helpful! A later assessment of the relationship between the Evangelicals and the government during this period was given by a Communist historian: "The Evangelical Christians, together with the Baptists, were the most moderate bourgeois reformative wing of sectarianism. Even the Tsarist government, which did not like in general any departures from Orthodox Christianity, did not apply any particular repression." [16] The leaders were not persecuted but some rank-and-file members were. "Intercession for the Evangelicals persecuted by local government brought before the Ministry of Internal Affairs almost always was successful."[17]

A great window of opportunity had opened for the Evangelical Christians. Prokhanov moved quickly to gain a permit for a religious periodical. This was granted in November of 1905. Prokhanov sent out the test number of the first Protestant paper in Russia in the same month. In January 1906 the first issue of *The Christian* was published. It carried Prokhanov's article, "On the Urgent Problems of the Evangelical Church in Russia." The paper continued for twenty-two years, with interruptions at the time of the Revolution and the Civil War, "until stopped by atheists." Each issue carried on the front page this slogan: "In essential things, unity. In secondary things, freedom. In all things, charity." Three objectives directed the publication: (1) the revelation to the Russian people of the substance of Christianity, which was the living Christ and nothing save Christ; (2) the evangelization of the Russian people; (3) the unification of all the branches of living Christianity. Prokhanov claimed that "during its existence, *The Christian* was...never influenced or carried away by politics or by any controversy. It never criticized or censured any Christian group or any religious worker."[18] Indeed, the periodical stressed

Christian living and maintained a positive, optimistic outlook throughout, which was remarkable given the later troubles. Each publication contained a hymn, many composed by Prokhanov, who continued to be the paper's editor until its demise.

Prokhanov had a respect for the printed word as did his predecessor, Pashkov. Supplements were added: the "Young Vineyard" for the youth, "The Brothers' Leaflet," "The Children's Library," and "New Melody." Other songbooks were published in addition to several editions of *Gusli*.[19] With publishing demands increasing, Prokhanov formed in 1908, in partnership with Heinrich Brown, a leader among the Mennonite Brethren, the publishing company Raduga ("The Rainbow"). Prokhanov proudly described this venture as "the first Protestant Christian publishing association in Russia."[20] Brown saw to the printing and finances, and Prokhanov produced the materials to be published. A store by the same name was opened in St. Petersburg. Soon large amounts of printed material were flowing to the people. In 1910, the biweekly newspaper, *The Morning Star*, was launched. A pocket-sized Bible was produced.

Among several works that Prokhanov authored, one, *A Short Treatise on Preaching*, printed in 1911, recorded the lectures he gave to the preachers' meetings in St. Petersburg. A portion, translated by Louis Patmont, gives an insight into Prokhanov's values.

> God has not forsaken us yet, and has not left us without His presence. The Russian people have received the Bread of Life, in spite of the fact that they were not allowed to read the truth and the Word of God was forbidden them for a century. We have had experience in Russia, a pure evangelical revival, and are approaching the restoration of undefiled Christian preaching....
>
> We all should rejoice and be thankful to God that

the movement has taken a scriptural form and that new churches are formed according to the spreading of the gospel....

To accomplish the reunion of all disciples (believers) we must apply one of the greatest of Christian weapons, prayer....

The divine Christ has been breaking the bonds of ignorance, weakness and oppression and opened a way to light and liberty and power, using as his channels and instruments his followers who, united through the harmony of love, grew in numbers and influence despite all exterior oppressions.[21]

The disposition toward centralization was long-standing in Russia. Indeed, the vastness of the country and the disparity among the regions seemed to call for schemes of central control.[22] It is understandable that Prokhanov, a gifted organizer and an engineer for whom order and organization were essential, was drawn to this model. He envisioned the linkage of independent congregations of Evangelical Christians through unions of conferences and their coordination through central councils. His first step was to organize the young people. Clearly, the youth held the key to the future of the movement. Before the decrees of toleration, the young adults had also met in secret. Prokhanov called for an organizational meeting on January 9, 1905. During their meeting they heard the cannons and rifle volleys which turned that day into "Bloody Sunday." Prokhanov, nevertheless, spoke prophetically of the coming day of religious liberty, of the rapid growth of the Evangelical Christians, and of the day when unions would combine their efforts. A "little union" would be established for the associations of Russian Christian young people. Within the year, the religious freedom came, as he predicted. The first congress of young Evangelical Christians and Baptists was held April 13, 1908, in Moscow. A union of the youth groups was formed, and Prokhanov was elected president of its council.

A vision of a "big union" of Evangelical congregations was also in Prokhanov's mind. As early as mid-1907, he had drafted proposed bylaws for such a union. These were confirmed by the Ministry of Internal Affairs by May of 1908. From Christmas Day in 1908 until January 7, 1909, a group met to organize the union and to elect its council. The first All-Russia Congress of the Evangelical Christians convened in St. Petersburg September 14-19, 1909. Twenty-four delegates, representing eighteen churches, along with thirty guests were present. Prokhanov explained the small numbers that gathered as the result of "some confusion" and the absence of congregational connections.[23] The meeting stipulated that all decisions were to be accepted only as advice for the congregations involved. Good Friday was designated as a day for fasting and prayer for the unity of God's people. It was determined to establish a Bible institute in St. Petersburg. The unity of Christian youth, singing, and children's meetings were considered. The congress officially formed the All-Russia Union of Evangelical Christians.

In all, ten congresses were convened under Prokhanov's leadership. The second and third congresses were called before the dislocations of the age settled in: the second, December 28, 1910, to January 4, 1911, with forty-seven delegates; the third, December 31, 1911, to January 4, 1912, with ninety-one delegates. A fourth congress, scheduled for 1913, was canceled by the government.[24] This congress finally met in 1917 and was followed by six more before Communist prohibition in 1928.

The first congress determined to send out a missionary named Alexander Persianov, who was directed to Siberia with his support set at 400 rubles. When a cry arose, "Where is the money?" Prokhanov responded, "Soon there will be five hundred missionaries in the field!" By 1928 there were indeed over five hundred active missionaries deployed.[25] Prokhanov stated the goal, "Every Evangelical Christian must be a missionary," and declared the slogan, "From city to city, from town to town, from village to village, from man to man." He encouraged the local churches to get out their maps and mark the places where there were not Evangelical churches. "Actually, we began to spiritually conquer the whole of Russia, and would have covered the whole territory but for the interference of atheism."[26] One source reports ten thousand Evangelical Christians and eleven thousand Baptists in Russia in 1910.[27]

In the second congress, the bylaws of the Union were presented and approved. It was stressed again that all churches of the Union were independent. The second congress acceded, however, to an unexpected initiative by Prokhanov. He wrote and submitted "The Confession of Faith of Evangelical Christians." He stated his reasoning. "At the time I thought very much about the necessity to create a strong basis for the unity of the whole movement. All of us recognized the New Testament as our only guide in our faith and our spiritual life, and have remained true to it until now, but for our practical work we needed to have a certain expression of the main bases of our faith."[28] The conference unanimously accepted and approved the "Confession."[29]

In the third congress, discussions were held on children's education, ordination, women in the churches, marriage, and divorce. It was determined that all believers should be involved in the singing of hymns, not just those in choirs.[30] The centralizing initiatives responded to the new freedoms in the land. Prokhanov's strategy enabled a vigorous response to the growing wave of defections from the state Church, and the Evangelicals grew rapidly.

The next step in Prokhanov's master plan was the establishment of a Bible college. No such institution had existed in Orthodox Russia. Even with the changes prospects were dim—except to the optimistic, aggressive Prokhanov! As early as December 1905, two-month training courses had been offered with Prokhanov, I. V. Kargel, Baron Paul Nicolay, and others instructing.[31] While useful, these short courses merely whetted Prokhanov's appetite for a full-fledged school. From 1905 on he repeatedly submitted applications to the government. Finally, in July 1912 the Ministry of Public Education gave approval. A fall opening was desired, but due to shortage of funds the beginning was postponed to avoid jeopardizing the charter. Two men, Alexander Persianov and Professor Martin Schmidt, were sent to America to seek assistance. The result was the mutual "discovery" of the Russian Evangelical Christians and the Christian Church (Disciples of Christ) in America.

The Disciples of Christ descended from a major effort in North America during the nineteenth century to restore New Testament Christianity. The principles that drove this movement found their parallels in the Russian experience: a return to the simple practice of the disciples of the New Testament, the rejection of a denominational expression of Christianity in favor of the unity of all believers in honor of Christ and his prayer for unity, and a respect for the Bible as the only authority in religion. The affinities between the Russian Evangelicals and the American Disciples prompted thoughts of alignment and shared efforts.

In fact, the connections between the two groups had been in place for some time. Z. T. Sweeney, a prominent Disciples minister, had learned of the Russian evangelical awakening in 1898 in Constantinople while serving as the American consul-general to Turkey.[32] Ivan Ivanovich, a Pashkovite, and his father, had been exiled to the Transcaucasus in 1892. Ivan arrived in America in 1903 after eleven years of exile. His name anglicized to become John Johnson, he was baptized in 1904 and in that year opened the Russian Christian Mission in New York City. The mission became a church in 1908 and identified with the Christian Church in 1910. William Durban, a Disciple in London acquainted with William Fetler, placed an article titled "Why Not Evangelize Russia?" in the Disciples' paper, The Christian-Evangelist of February 1909. Thus the story of the Russian Evangelical awakening was known by key leaders in the Christian Church in America.

Russian awareness of the American group had also developed. Persianov, during his missionary journeys in Siberia, had met Johnson's father, who related his son's activities in America. Persianov and Johnson then exchanged correspondence in 1909. Timothy Davidov, formerly an elder in the Russian Christian Church in New York and now a missionary in Russia, attended the third congress of the Evangelical Christians. When a telegram of greeting to the congress arrived from I. N. McCash, secretary of the American Christian Missionary Society (ACMS), and Joseph Keevil of the Disciples' Mission Union, Davidov arose to explain who the American Disciples were. Keevil followed this with a January 12, 1912, letter to Prokhanov, in which he questioned Prokhanov concerning his faith and practices. Prokhanov responded promptly and offered to send representatives to America to attend the Disciples' national convention. When the approval for the Bible college was received in July of 1912, Prokhanov had added incentive to follow through on his proposal.

Persianov and Schmidt traveled to America and attended the annual meeting of the ACMS in Louisville, Kentucky, in the fall of 1912.[33] They traveled and spoke for three months but were not successful in raising any funds. On the eve of Schmidt's departure back to Russia, several interested Disciples formed a Special Russian Emergency Committee with Z. T. Sweeney as chairman. This group pledged to raise the needed money for the St. Petersburg Bible school and set a goal of $5,000. "It would be," he said, "a mark of our brotherly appreciation to help them in their extremity to save their Bible college, and it would serve to bind together the Christians in the two countries.[34] Later he reported, "There is no doubt that these Evangelical Christians of Russia are our own spiritual kith and kin. They are the disciples of Christ of Russia."[35]

Sweeney, accompanied by Lois R. Patmont who served as translator, traveled to Russia in April and May 1913 to gain firsthand impressions of the Russian "restoration." They visited the Evangelicals' congregations in both St. Petersburg and Moscow, reporting memberships of nine hundred and seven hundred, respectively. Sweeney estimated that the Evangelical Christians across Russia numbered approximately 100,000. Thirty-six evangelists served in a field that stretched six thousand miles. Sweeney came away much impressed. In his special report to the American Disciples that appeared in the July 3, 1913, issue of the *Christian Standard*, he stated: "...the Gospel Christians are as emphatic and insistent upon New Testament Christianity as the Christians of the United States."[36] The American Disciples, however, did not rally to Sweeney's appeal for the $50,000 that would supply a large building for the school and permit graduation of "a hundred preachers a year" for Russian evangelism. During 1913, a little over $5,000 was transferred to the Evangelical Christian's college initiative.[37]

The assurance of support from America, however, allowed Prokhanov to launch the Bible school on February 27, 1912. Notice of the formal opening appeared in the *Morning Star*. It begins, "On February 14 (old style), at 10:30 a.m. at the central place of meeting of the Evangelical Christian Church [Danishev's Gymnasium on Fonarny Pereul], the College of the Bible was formally opened on the basis of the charter granted by the Department of Education."[38] Nine students enrolled in the school, situated at Thirteen First Reia. Prokhanov was president and main teacher along with teachers A. A. Reimer and G. K. Inkis. The school opened for its second term on September 13, 1913; nineteen students were admitted from the many who applied. Sadly, the school was short-lived. The declaration of war in August 1914 brought it and other initiatives of the Evangelical Christians to a standstill.

More immediate trouble loomed for the Evangelicals: persecution broke out once again. The Duma had represented a leadership alternative to the imperial regime which both propped up and exploited the state Church. The first Duma, April 22 to July 6, 1906, stood for the right of all dissenters to organize congregations and churches. Yet both the first and the second Dumas, active from February 7 through June 1907, served for limited durations. The third Duma was in place from November 1907 until 1911, its members chosen under Prime Minister Stolypin's election law. This body recognized the October 1905 Manifesto; thus the majority party was known as the October Party. The Duma defended the rights of the people from the abuses which had been perpetrated by the old regime. This explains, in part, Prokhanov's success in his printing, organizational, and educational initiatives. When he could not get satisfaction from the Tsarist Department of Religious Affairs, he would apply to the Duma's Committee on Religious Cults. Kamensky, the president of the Committee was sympathetic to the Evangelical movement.

The brief respite from the Church's bitter treatment had enabled major advances for the believers in Russia. Prokhanov's leadership gave new meaning to the adage, "Work, for the night is coming!" His bold and shrewd dealings with the various governing bodies, pressing every reasonable advantage, gave the entire nation a glimpse, if just for a moment, of what freedom and "optimism"—Prokhanov's favorite word— might mean. His work was prodigious. On the eve of the reversals in 1911 and 1912, he was editing the biweekly newspaper, the monthly church paper and its several supplements, often composing a hymn per month. He preached weekly, morning and evening, often at the large Terishevsky Hall in the center of the city. He presided at weekly meetings of the church council and the regular meetings of the "large" and "small" unions. His correspondence and involvement with Evangelicals across Russia, including tracking the efforts of the traveling evangelists, was extensive. All the while, he maintained his regular job as a mechanical engineer with the Westinghouse Air Brake Company. He later reminisced:

> I usually worked until 2 o'clock in the morning and had far too little rest, but the urge and necessity of the Evangelical work impelled me, and surely the strength of the Lord was provided to meet my needs. Hard as I labored, I felt bright, strong and cheerful, and my mind was continually full of new ideas and projects vital

and necessary to all branches of my work. The daily habit of doing all things according to a written program was most valuable at this period of my life.[39]

By 1911 however, Orthodox voices began to speak more and more loudly, insisting on stronger measures to limit the dissenters. On October 4, the Minister of Interior issued a rule that limited the freedom of religious expression and narrowed the principles of the decrees of April and October 1905 and of October 1906. Meetings of religious bodies were restricted. Permission to hold special meetings was required from the police two weeks in advance. Religious instruction of those under twenty-one was prohibited. A police officer was required to be present at all meetings. The senate in December 1912 limited preaching and movement. Some leaders were convicted in the lower courts. The instigator of these repressive moves was the priestly party under the leadership of the nefarious Rasputin. Two telegrams received in America detail some of the actions taken.

> **St. Petersburg, Dec. 18, 1912**—The Holy Orthodox Synod has turned its persecution upon Christians and Baptists, whose places of worship are now being stamped out by the political secret service police, in just the same fashion as the Jews were hounded out and driven into the pale. Prayer-houses in Livland and other provinces have been suddenly raided and closed with police padlocks, by order of the Government, which places them in the same category as conspirator's clubs. M. Sabler, Procurator of the Holy Synod, declared roundly that any form of worship in Russia that is not under the discipline of the Orthodox Church has the same danger to the Czar as a revolutionary conspiracy to the

state.

Omsk, Siberia, Dec. 16, 1912—Persecution of baptized Christians has been resumed by the authorities. A colony of industrious farmers have been evicted from their lands because of their religious beliefs. Some of the Government ministers have failed to abate the persecutions, as the Czar is more under the sway of the fanatical religionists.[40]

Germany's declaration of war against Russia gave further excuse for the state to bring restrictive measures upon nonconforming Russians. The reactionary party in the Church exploited the times. Shortly the persecutors would become the persecuted, but under this final attack the evangelicals suffered as before the Manifesto. A great number of Evangelical Christian elders and Baptist pastors were banished to Siberia. The publication of both *The Christian* and *Morning Star* was suspended. Meetings in St. Petersburg and across Russia were forbidden. The Bible school was closed. Neither the Evangelical nor Baptist union was permitted to conduct congresses or conferences. Many evangelicals were conscientious objectors, and this aggravated official censure. Prokhanov was indicted in the lower court for "revolutionary union organization," but he was never summoned. The anti-German sentiment during the war lumped the Evangelicals with the Stundists and accused them of fostering a "German religion."[41] Prokhanov, who remained in Russia throughout the war, stressed the Russian essence of the Evangelicals. He also pointed to the movement's early English influences, such as Radstock, Müller, and Baedeker. Having friends in high places also helped to shield them somewhat from the prejudices of the day.

The years immediately ahead would be filled with unimaginable human suffering—the years of the

Great War, the Communist Revolution, the Russian Civil War, and famine. But in the midst of these terrors for a brief, tantalizing decade, the "Golden Age of the Evangelicals" was about to dawn.

---

[1] Four Dumas assembled before the Bolshevik Revolution. Their legislation was subject to imperial approval.

[2] In his autobiography *In the Cauldron of Russia, 1869-1933* (Joplin, MO: College Press, 1993), Prokhanov does not identify whether these "believers" are Molokans, Baptists, Stundists, or Evangelicals.

[3] A method of printing which uses a slab of gelatin treated with glycerin.

[4] Prokhanov, 75.

[5] Prokhanov, 79.

[6] Prokhanov, 93.

[7] Prokhanov, 104.

[8] "[T]he foundation of the Russian state remained the threefold principle, *Orthodoxy, Autocracy, Nationalism.* State and Orthodoxy were tightly connected." S. Melginov, *Church and State in Russia* (Moscow, 1907), quoted in *History of the Evangelical Christian-Baptists of the USSR* (Moscow, 1989; portions translated from Russian by Lydia Loginova), 135.

[9] Prokhanov, 130-31.

[10] *History of Evangelical Christian-Baptists*, 133.

[11] Prokhanov, 135.

[12] Gregory L. Nichols, "Pashkovism: Nineteenth-Century Russian Piety," master's thesis, Wheaton College Graduate School, 1991, 73.

[13] E. H. Broadbent, *The Pilgrim Church* (London: Pickering and Inglis Ltd., 1st ed., 1931; 4th ed., 1950), 336.

[14] The second to be registered was the Second Christian Church of St. Petersburg, under I. Kargel's direction. Fetler led in registering the Baptist Church of St. Petersburg.

[15] Elders were evidently in place as well, but direction of the affairs of the congregation was provided by the council.

[16] A. Yartsev, *The Cult of Evangelical Christians* (Moscow: Atheist Publishing House, 4th Completely Reviewed Edition, 1930; translated from Russian by Yuri Dobrokotov), 6.

[17] Yartsev, 6.

[18] Prokhanov, 139.

[19] The 1909 edition of *Gusli* contained 507 songs. In 1910 Raduga published *New Harp*, a book of hymns and poems. Ten songbooks in all, including 1443 songs (624 by Prokhanov, 406 by other Russian composers, 413 from other sources; Prokhanov, 146).

[20] Prokhanov, 148.

[21] Quoted in *The Christian-Evangelist*, April 17, 1913.

[22] All-Russia Unions were commonplace, e.g., the All-Russia Union of Soviets (1917), the All-Russia Union of Baptists.

[23] Prokhanov, 149.

[24] Prokhanov attributed the government's refusal to issue further permits to its growing awareness of the success of the Union. (Prokhanov, 151).

[25] Prokhanov, 152.

[26] Prokhanov, 154-55.

[27] Yartsev, 8.

[28] Prokhanov, 155.

[29] Prokhanov did not see this as a significant move away from the Evangelical Christians' commitment to "the Bible only."

[30] One of the guests at the third congress was the eighty-year-old Michael Ratushny, the first Russian Stundist. *(Christian Standard*, April 26, 1913).

[31] See Greta Langenskjold and Baron Paul Nicolay, *Christian Statesmen and Student Leaders in Northern and Slavic Europe* (New York: George H. Doran Company, 1924; tr. Ruth Evelyn Wilder).

[32] *The Christian Standard*, July 3, 1886.

[33] Prokhanov also traveled to Louisville and spoke at the 1912 ACMS convention. He does not record this visit in his autobiography, and the Disciples' papers give only passing reference to his travels in America, cf. *The Christian-Evangelist*, July 3, 1913.

[34] *The Christian-Evangelist*, Jan. 23, 1913.

[35] *Christian Century*, Jan. 31, 1913.

[36] *Christian Standard*, 1891.

[37] Eighteen articles concerning the Russian opportunity appeared in the American Disciples' church papers, *The Christian Standard* and *The Christian-Evangelist*, during the first seven months of 1913, fourteen written by Louis Patmont.

[38] Z. T. Sweeney, George W. Kramer, A. U. Chaney, and C. B. Drake, "Opening Exercises of the Bible College at St. Petersburg," *Christian Standard*, March 22, 1913, 10, tr. John Johnson.

[39] Prokhanov, 158.

40 *Christian Standard*, January 11, 1913; 5.

41 Skvortsov, leader among the "Missionaries," i.e. Orthodox opponents of dissenters, and a member of the Holy Synod, charged, "A whole number of factual documentary evidence appeared that stundo-baptism and sectarian Evangelicals have anti-state dogmas in the foundation of their teaching, and followers of the cult show themselves obvious traitors to the Tsar and Fatherland at war and are friends of the Teutons." *Kolokol* ("*The Bell*"), Feb. 22, 1915. Y-5, 7.

II

The other Revolution

It is ironic that the Russian Evangelicals made greater advances during the first decade of Communist power than they had during their first four decades under the repression of the state church. The Bolsheviks seized control of the country during a period of extreme instability brought on by the collapsing imperial regime and the failing war effort. The Tsar's conduct increasingly alienated him from his people. He handled the 1905 uprisings poorly. His family succumbed to the influences of the fanatical Rasputin. He resisted the Duma's push to constitutional monarchy. In 1915 Nicholas II insisted on personally taking over the direction of the war effort and consequently took the blame for its failures and frustrations. The previously unthinkable slogan "Down with the Tsar!" was heard across the land.

The demands of war all too graphically revealed the deficiencies of Russian society. The dislocation of industry and transportation for the war effort resulted in food shortages, inflation, and hunger, destabilizing the government.[1] The Bolshevik Revolution, which a hundred years of abuse and reaction made all but inevitable, began in February 1917 as a spontaneous people's protest. The Duma refused to step down at the

Tsar's March 12th command. Upon Nicholas II's abdication on March 15, the Duma formed the Provisional Government.[2] At the same time, the revolutionaries in Petrograd[3] established the first people's "Soviet."[4] Initially the Petrograd Soviet and the Provisional Government cooperated as the latter sought to redress the glaring wrongs of the past.[5] In the meantime the peasants seized the remaining landed estates.

Into the confusion entered Lenin, coming by sealed train from Germany and arriving at the Finland Station in Petrograd on April 2, 1917.[6] His "April Theses," given the next day, called for Russia's withdrawal from the war, the end of the Provisional Government, and "all power to the soviets." He demanded that the land and banks be nationalized. During the next six months, the Bolsheviks strengthened their hold and were emboldened to launch "The Revolution" on October 29.[7] After the success of the bloodless coup which overthrew the Provisional Government, Lenin moved to implement the plan he had announced. The Church was disestablished, and education was taken over by the state. Negotiations for peace were begun. Private property was abolished, and the holdings of the Crown, the Church, and monasteries were expropriated. The Soviet ratified peace with Germany in the costly and humiliating Treaty of Brest-Litovsk on March 16, 1918.[8]

Opposition to the "Red" Bolsheviks developed throughout Russia, and foreign interests attempted to intervene. Russia was plunged into civil war as the counter-revolutionaries, "The Whites," raised armies and marched on the heartland from the east, the south and the northwest. One by one, the Reds' challengers were eliminated. Russia's former allies from WWI launched expeditions with minimal effect.[9] By 1921, pressures required that the Bolsheviks abandon their policy of "War Communism" and retreat somewhat from their forced socialist approaches. A "New Economic Policy" was implemented. In place of the Tsars' forced requisition of grain, farmers were taxed. Private enterprise was permitted. At the Party Congress in March 1921, Lenin ruled out any dissent within the Communist Party.[10] Totalitarianism was now entrenched. By the end of 1922, the Bolsheviks had consolidated their power from Moscow in the west to Vladivostok, "the last stronghold of the Whites," in the far east.[11]

During the period of the Civil War, 1918-1922, agricultural production tumbled, industrial activity came almost to a standstill, and the distress was deepened by a drought in the southern region (1920-21) with a net result of five million deaths. "Altogether, the seven years of war, civil war, famine, and starvation left Russia with a population deficit of about twenty-eight million."[12]

Prokhanov described this period as "an appalling reign of terror." Revolutionary tribunals were established that had as their aim the annihilation of the leaders of the bourgeoisie and men of influence; thousands of officers were killed, a number drowned; many clergymen of the Church were shot; and numbers of the aristocracy were killed; including Tsar Nicholas and his family at Ekaterinburg in the Urals. Prokhanov reported, "According to official figures, which were published from 1917 through 1922 in the Soviet press from day to day, a total of about 1,800,000 executions took place, including 28 archbishops, 1,400 priests and 8,800 doctors."[13] Rumors were rampant. "One day a report spread that all priests, pastors, preachers, and active religious workers would be shot." Another day, "a brother came to my house and said I. S. Prokhanov was sentenced to be shot. I awaited a visit of the executioners during weeks, but they never came."[14]

Prokhanov sent his wife and two sons away from Petrograd to Tiflis in the Transcaucasus, but Anna Ivanovna died of cholera at Vladikavkas on July 30, 1919. Prokhanov's apartment of five rooms was frigid, with "only the kitchen a little heated." He slept in a room "in which the windows were frozen, clad in [his] felt boots and wearing a fur coat and a fur hat." Food was very scarce. For an extended period Prokhanov survived on carrot tea and dry bread, "morning, noon and night." "Nevertheless, I didn't discontinue my work even for a day."[15]

The growing terror of Bolshevism, clearly comprehended in retrospect, could only be imagined in the disturbed days of 1917. What was clear then was that the terrors of the imperial regime were at an end. Indeed, an era of some hopefulness had dawned. Prokhanov recalled his early attitude: "Inasmuch as we saw social and economic reforms in the revolution we welcomed it. To some extent we saw in it God's judgment upon the guilty. Or else we considered it a purification [from] which Russia must come forth renewed."[16] Following the initial stage of the revolution, on February 17, 1917 an amnesty was declared for all convicted of religious crimes, and people returned to their families. The Provisional Government struggled with the issue of the separation of church and state. At the invitation of President Kerensky, Prokhanov addressed the Moscow State Conference on August 17, 1917. He stressed that the nation could only be purified by the emancipation of the state church and the equalization of rights for all religions and faiths.

It was left to the Bolsheviks, however, to accomplish this major change. On January 27, 1918, the decree was issued to separate the church from the state and education from the church. The decree stated that everyone was free to confess any religion or no religion.

However, religious learning could be received only privately, and churches could not hold property or be treated before the law as a person. The thirteenth paragraph of the Constitution of the USSR stated, "In order to ensure for the workers true freedom of conscience, the church is separated from the state and the school from the church, and freedom of religious and anti-religious propaganda is guaranteed for every citizen of the Republic."[17] Following years of oppression, the Evangelicals were delivered—by the Bolsheviks!—into a period of relative freedom of action. However, Prokhanov judged, "I knew that these favorable laws would have power only for a certain time and that they would be followed by restrictions at least, and therefore I decided to use this temporary religious liberty by laboring to our utmost capacity in preaching the gospel, to which intensive program I invited all my fellow workers."[18]

Prokhanov, methodical as always, planned his strategy for the immediate future, as uncertain as it might be. He returned to his preaching and publishing, renewed the congresses of the All-Russia Union of Evangelical Christians, revived preacher-training efforts, advanced the organizational structure of the Union, printed Bibles and hymnbooks, explored an alliance with the Baptists and rapprochement with the Orthodox Church, encouraged the youth movement, experimented with collectives, and pondered a worldwide, nondenominational union of Evangelicals.

Prokhanov returned on March 12, 1917, to preaching at Tenishev's Hall in St. Petersburg, where he had preached before 1915. At one special meeting at the circus of Chiniselli, he addressed three thousand on "The Spiritual Revolution." Parades were staged from Tenishev's Hall to the Marine Menage (equestrian hall), which had a seating capacity of ten thousand. "Those were grand meetings."[19] Similar meetings spread to other cities—Moscow, Saratov, Kharkov, Kiev, and Odessa. Preaching took place in the squares, streets, parks, halls, universities, and institutes. After the war concluded, several thousand soldiers returned as believers and took their lot with the Evangelicals and the Baptists.[20] A revival was underway.

The publication of *The Christian* and the *Morning Star* was revived, but on poorer paper due to the shortages and sporadically because of emerging tensions in the country. During 1919, it was possible to publish only eight issues of the *Morning Star,* and *The Christian* was not published again until 1923. By 1927, *The Christian* reached a circulation of 15,000.

Congresses of the All-Russia Union of Evangelical Christians were held once again. Between 1917 and 1921 five congresses were held, alternating between Petrograd and Moscow. The ninth and tenth congresses were held in Petrograd[21] in 1923 and 1926. These gatherings give an insight into the concerns of the Evangelicals and their developments during the first decade of Communist rule.

The fourth congress, prohibited by the Tsarist government in 1913, took place May 17-25, 1917, while the Provisional Government was still in power. One hundred delegates, plus Baptist representatives such as Vasili Pavlov and M. D. Timoshenko, managed to attend. During the deliberations, Prokhanov proposed that the congress approve the formation of the Resurrection Party, a coalition of Christian Democrats. The congress declined, not wanting the churches to become involved in politics.[22] Prokhanov, however, proceeded on his own and became the Christian-Democrat candidate for the Petrograd district in the November 1917 constituent assembly election held by the All-Russian Congress of Soviets. Prokhanov received more votes than the Social Democrats ("Mensheviks"), but fewer than the Constitutional Democrats ("Cadets") and the

Bolsheviks. The newly elected assembly met in January 1918 only to be shut down by the Bolsheviks, who had received only 25% of the overall votes. "Russia had experienced just one day of revolutionary democracy."[23]

The final six congresses of the Evangelical Christians were convened by the permission of Soviet authorities. The four held during the civil war were attended by 94, 90, 15, and 142 delegates, respectively. The last two, the ninth and tenth congresses of 1923 and 1926, received 303 and 503 delegates. The fifth congress, held shortly after the Bolshevik Revolution, had as its slogan, "The hour has come for you to wake up from your sleep" (Romans 13:11). The consistent theme of these gatherings was the spreading of the good news. Fifty preachers were sent out from the sixth congress and one hundred from the eighth. The seventh congress sent missionaries to India, China, and to different nationalities living within Russia. Later congresses gave attention to relations with the new political masters, to preacher training, and to unity with the Baptists. The congresses reflected a rapidly growing movement during quickly changing times.

Unity of believers was an ever-present interest of Prokhanov. In this he grasped the biblical imperative and stood in the tradition of Pashkov, who earlier had worked for the unification of the Russian evangelicals. The evangelical awakening in Russia had gradually consolidated into two major groupings, the Evangelical Christians and the Baptists. Many felt that a merger was a logical move since both practiced the immersion of adults, upheld congregational integrity, and respected the Bible as the only authority. One of the goals stated at the formation of the All-Russia Evangelical Christian Union in 1909 was "To bring to the Union all who seek the truth." Prokhanov stated in 1910, "Now it is very important to think about unity. The evangelical movement has as its goal the renewal of the religious life of the Russian people. And for this purpose it is necessary to unite all branches...."[24] Prior to the Revolution, neither group was ready for the move. The Baptists were not in agreement with Prokhanov's emphasis on social regeneration. The Evangelicals were not enthusiastic about the Baptist's perceived restrictive doctrines. During this earlier period Prokhanov encouraged shared ventures in youth work, evangelism, and preacher training, but not outright union with the Baptists. This did not stop him, however, from having the Evangelical Christian Union join the World Baptist Union nor from accepting the position of one of ten vice-presidents of that association in 1911.[25]

After 1917 Prokhanov supported full merger. "Unity" returned to the agenda of the sixth Evangelical congress in 1919. Ten delegates were appointed to represent the Evangelicals in a temporary union with the Baptists. A united Temporary All-Russia General Council met January 19-24, 1920, and issued this resolution: "According to the Savior's will for God's children to be united, it is necessary to call all believers, Evangelical Christians and Baptists, to strain every nerve...for merging two unions in one."[26] The council published its own magazine, *Brothers United*, with the motto "And join them one to another into one stick, and they shall become one in your hand" (Ezekiel 37:17). Preparations were made for the upcoming congress of May 27-June 7 in Moscow, the seventh congress of the Evangelical Christians to run concurrently with the Baptist congress.[27] By May 29 the delegates concluded that there were no essential differences in doctrine or life practices between the two groups,[28] and agreement to merge was reached. Some practical considerations intervened, however. The first question was where to locate the council of the All-Russia Union of Evangelical Christians and Baptists: Moscow or Petrograd? The second question was to determine who would lead. The

Evangelicals wanted Prokhanov to be president with a Baptist vice-president at Petrograd; the Baptists wanted a collegial presidency with the council located in Moscow.[29] These unresolved issues were sufficient to defeat the unity initiative. The question returned at the eighth and ninth Evangelical congresses, December 1921 and September 1923, but no advance was realized.[30] In 1925 disagreement over the joint leadership of the Bible college resulted in the withdrawal of Baptist funding and the termination of further attempts at union.

A significant point of difference between the two groups in practice, and reflecting a contrasting view of ministry, was the matter of ordination. "Laying on of hands" was practiced by the Baptists but not by the Evangelicals. This was an agenda item for meetings of the Evangelical Christian congresses—the third, of January 1912, and the eighth, of December 1921. However, Prokhanov, while on tour in Czechoslovakia had accepted ordination by a Baptist pastor in Prague on April 1. From that time the practice was followed by the Russian Evangelicals.

That Prokhanov was serious about spiritual reformation of the nation is demonstrated in his remarkable initiative with the former oppressor, the Orthodox Church. Both the disestablishment in 1918 and the severe treatment by the Soviet government during the Civil War resulted in considerable instability within the Church. In 1922, the state confiscated all valuables, gold, silver, and precious stones from the churches, temples, mosques, and monasteries—ostensibly to feed the starving masses. On the same day of the government's decree, the Church banned surrender of any sacramental objects, giving rise to severe repression.[31] Tikhon (Belavin), Metropolitan of Moscow and Patriarch of the Church—the patriarchate having been restored in 1917—was placed under house arrest on May 6, 1922.[32] The Church was off-balance and wracked with multiple schisms. Collectively known as the "Renovationists," the schismatics included three branches: the "Living Church" with Krasnitzky as leader, the "Ancient Apostolic Church" with leader Bishop Vvedensky, and the "Church of Regeneration" under Metropolitan Antonin. Together, these *Obnovlenzi* ("Renewers"), led by progressive priests and exploited by the government, formed the "Supreme Council of the Greek Orthodox Church" and presumed to govern the whole Church.

Disestablishment of the Church, however, was not uniformly unpopular among the priests and laypersons of Orthodoxy. Many welcomed the release of the Church from the secularizing embrace of the state and hoped for its spiritual revival. To these and to all the Orthodox, Prokhanov directed a special appeal, "The Gospel Call." The writing contained three points: (1) The Evangelical Christians forgave the Orthodox persecutors of their offenses. (2) The Orthodox clergy was urged to begin a national New Testament-based reformation. (3) The Evangelical Christians would arrange special prayer meetings in Moscow and Petrograd, which Orthodox believers of all persuasions were invited to attend, to seek God's help for this reform. One hundred thousand copies of "The Gospel Call" were distributed with great effect across Russia.

In Moscow, Prokhanov was invited to preach in an Orthodox cathedral. In his remarks he stated, "Behold, brothers and sisters, today a miracle has happened before my very eyes! More than thirty years ago, I said in St. Petersburg that we would have the chance to preach the gospel in the Orthodox Church. No one believed me at the time—and today it has come to pass!"[33] Prokhanov spoke on the nature of the gospel and urged the Russian people to repent. The attending priest responded in prayer, "Lord, forgive me as a simple sinner and as the sinner-shepherd of these immortal souls with regard to whom I was so neglectful."[34] Prokhanov then visited Metropolitan Antonin, who stated that he agreed with almost everything written in "The Gospel Call." "But this program can't be realized in the Greek Orthodox Church at present," he told Prokhanov. He then took a book from a shelf and said, "This is the book from which I am taking drops of living water every day." It was a copy of *Gusli*. Taking his leave from the Metropolitan, Prokhanov suggested that they pray together, which they did. Prokhanov remembers, "One of the brethren who accompanied me wept with tears of joy. Surely there was reason for his tears. It is certain that in a thousand years never such a thing happened as that a Metropolitan of the Greek Orthodox Church would pray in his own words with outsiders, yet here he prayed with the representatives of the people's Evangelical movement."[35] Later, in a religious gathering, Antonin was asked which church or religious organization came nearest to the teachings of Christ. He responded, "I know one group of Christians: they are called Evangelical Christians. They restore the primitive Christianity of Christ and the apostles."[36] The special day of prayer for Orthodox revival and Russian reformation was set for November 1922. Metropolitan Antonin attended the Moscow meeting and gave an address. Word of these remarkable meetings spread across Russia and the attitudes of the Orthodox regarding the Evangelicals "changed altogether...."[37]

Later, Prokhanov was invited by the Ancient Apostolic Church schism to speak to its congress, scheduled for March 15, 1923. Prokhanov, the first to speak, was granted an hour. He again urged and prayed for the spiritual regeneration of Russia and received an enthusiastic response. "The social and spiritual influence of our Union at this time gained its highest level, manifesting its spiritual power upon these new efforts of the progressive elements of the Greek

Orthodox Church...."[38]

In the end, however, Prokhanov's efforts to move the Orthodox Church toward reformation were ineffectual, and they were not without cost to the Evangelical movement. While a number of priests altered their positions, Prokhanov's initiative was linked primarily with the schismatics. Orthodox habits of complicity with the state were deep-seated; and when schism occurred, political alignment followed. The Renovationists held a *sobor* (council) in April 1923, during which they stripped Tikhon of his ecclesiastical titles. They also directed a message to Lenin, declaring loyalty to the "divinely appointed" revolutionary government, gaining them the label "The Red Council." Prokhanov's association with these groups which mixed politics and religion harmed the Evangelical movement in the minds of many.

While the period 1918-1928 was a "golden age" for the Evangelicals, this description must be understood in relative terms.[39] Communist antipathy to religion and its harsh treatment of the former state church, "a prop of Tsarism and a pillar of reaction," meant that increasingly persecution would come to the sectarians.[40] In Lenin's mind, "Every religious idea, every idea of God, even flirting with the idea of God, is unutterable vileness."[41] The Bolsheviks, during their early consolidation of power, viewed the evangelicals as worthy of wooing. At the Communists' twelfth Party Congress in 1923, it was acknowledged that the evangelicals had been "subjected to the most cruel persecution on the part of Tsarism."[42] Further, "Sectarians have considerable economic and cultural forces now to be tactfully channeled to Soviet work."[43] This gentler attitude was demonstrated by the government's early treatment of religious pacifists. Bonch-Bruevich, secretary to Lunacharsky, the People's Commissar of Education, persuaded Lenin and Trotsky to allow those with conscientious objection against bearing arms to serve alternatively in medical work.[44] The same man sat on a special committee established by the Commissariat of Agriculture to supply land for development by communities of Evangelical Christians, Baptists, and Old Believers.[45] Prokhanov led the Evangelicals in organizing the "Morning Star" community in Tver. A brotherhood-wide assistance program was organized to support the new cooperatives. But when it became evident that the believers were resistant to the Socialists' recruiting, they also fell under the government's heavy hand. Illustrative of this were the two arrests experienced by Prokhanov.

A youth conference was scheduled for Tver (now Kalinin) in 1921, to be hosted by Prokhanov.[46] On the third day of the gathering, a mob came with revolvers and jailed all forty-three participants. After ten days in the cells, during which time the agenda of the conference was concluded and the continuous singing and teaching by the prisoners became contagious, the group was released to await trial. The sentence consigned twelve, including Prokhanov, to three years' hard labor. The authorities intervened, however, and dropped the sentences, instead punishing the instigators for false arrest.

In 1923, pressure mounted for the Evangelicals to acknowledge the Soviet government. In the middle of a night in April, Prokhanov's house and offices were searched. At gun point, Prokhanov was forced to sign an agreement to appear in three days, along with his secretary, Dubrovsky, at the Moscow Cheka (political police) office. He was then arrested. It was Easter. For a number of days, they were left in the inner prison along with prisoners of every description. Prokhanov was required to draft a statement detailing the attitude of the Evangelical Christians toward the government. His reply, centered in Romans 13, was not satisfactory to the investigating judge. Repeated meetings, solitary confinement, and allegations of what "other" Evangelical Christians were supposedly agreeing to left Prokhanov weak, troubled, and uncertain. Eventually, he felt forced to give recognition to the government and to agree to participation in military service by his followers. He described his plight: "I was in a very depressed state and could only agree, in the hope that...the question would only be finally settled at an All-Russian congress."[47] The appeal accepted by the judge was examined by the ninth Evangelical congress of September 1-10, in St. Petersburg. It was agreed that according to Romans 13, the Soviet government had its purpose before God. Regarding military service, the resolution was accepted which stated, "We regard military duty, according to the laws in force, as an obligation, but we leave it to the individual Christian to act according to his conscience."[48] Prokhanov was set free. He concluded that with the clarification of the attitude of the Evangelical Christians toward the government, a position matched by the Baptists, "[the government] is satisfied and thanks to this, there are unlimited opportunities for evangelism. There is no more oppression; we can have meetings wherever and whenever we like. We can found fellowships and unions without difficulty."[49] It is to be remembered that these events took place during the last year of the life of Lenin, who was committed to rule by law.[50]

Prokhanov rebounded to vigorous activity to compensate for time lost in prison.[51] "This period, from 1923 to 1929, proved to be the most fruitful with regard to the work of our Evangelical movement through the Union. The publication work, Bible education and missionary efforts were facilitated by favorable laws passed by the Soviet Government."[52] No Bibles had been printed in Russia since 1914 by either the Evangelicals or the Orthodox Church. Following the Civil War, Bibles were secured from the European organization "Licht im Osten" ("Light in the East") through the British and Foreign Bible Society's office in Reval, capital of the still-free republic of Estonia. From this supply a quantity of Bibles and hymnals were received.[53] This source was closed in 1924, and the supply of Scriptures was soon exhausted. Prokhanov determined to visit America to seek funding for the Evangelicals' publishing needs and for humanitarian relief. His trip lasted from May 1925 until November 1926, and he arrived home just in time for the beginning of the tenth All-Russia Evangelical Christian Union congress. During his travels he raised $100,000. With these funds in hand, a total of 175,000 pieces were printed.[54] This great quantity of printing was accomplished by atheist printing establishments eager for the money. Ironically, throughout the period, Orthodox interests could not secure printing permits. Prokhanov observed, "The deep significance of this production and scattering over Russia of the word of God will be better understood and appreciated if one remembers that while there was a famine of Scripture, the whole of Russia was being flooded with atheistic literature all the time."[55]

Included in this mammoth printing enterprise were sixty thousand hymnbooks. Of this number, twenty-five thousand were the 1927 second edition of *Spiritual Songs,* plus ten thousand of this collection with notes added. Containing twelve hundred thirty-seven hymns, "the most complete songbook at that time,"[56] it was, in fact, the "collection of ten," or a compilation of ten earlier separate hymnbooks. In its foreword, Prokhanov introduced each of these sections with a brief commentary. One of the collections was *Songs of the First Christians.* His introduction stated that this section "was put together in such a way as to take the believers back to the first century of Christianity. This is not even necessary, because the evangelical movement in Russia today is a revival of original Christianity, that is, Christianity at the time of the apostles."[57]

How successful had the Russian endeavor been at restoring New Testament Christianity? A revised assessment by the American Disciples of Christ was forthcoming in mid-decade. As early as 1920, Prokhanov had sought American relief for the plight of the Russian believers caught in the aftermath of war and revolution and in so doing had revived his contacts with the Disciples. During this period, the Disciples had been encouraging the growth of Russian congregations in America, especially in New York and Chicago. Karl Borders, superintendent of Brotherhood House, a Russian-oriented community center in Chicago, went to Russia as a missionary and director of relief work for nine months during 1922 and 1923. At the end of this period, he traveled to Petrograd and Moscow to examine firsthand the Evangelical Christian movement. In the meantime, the Disciples had collected $65,000 for relief purposes through its "Men and Millions" movement but had determined to survey the Russian effort again, including the Bible college, before distributing the funds. Frederick W. Burnham and A. E. Cory were commissioned to go to Russia. Prokhanov arrived in America in late May 1925, a month before their departure, and was able to brief them in advance of their travels. Both Borders and Burnham submitted their conclusions in Disciples publications subsequent to their surveys.[58]

The American assessment was that the Russian Evangelical Christians were neither Baptists nor Disciples and, in significant points, were not fully restorationist according to American standards. The autonomy of the congregation was held to by both the East and the West, but the Russian Union was an

ecclesiastical organization in the Disciples' view. Respect
for the Bible as wholly inspired and the sole authority
was held by both, but the Evangelicals' adherence to
the Statement of Faith composed by Prokhanov had
creedal overtones. Both practiced adult baptism by
immersion, but the Evangelical Christians viewed this
practice in the same light as the Baptists—it was not for
the remission of sins. Both observed the Lord's Supper
as a communion, but the Evangelicals practiced a "semi-
closed" communion and did not observe it weekly. Both
selected elders, deacons and preachers, but the Russian
practice opted for a single elder in each church instead
of the American plurality, and local congregational
authority was vested in a council rather than centered
in the elder. Borders observed that the Evangelical
Christians were more Baptist than Disciple. Burnham
concluded, "The group must remain what it is now: a
Russian Evangelical body uncontrolled or dominated
by any religious force. These leaders appreciate the
liberty which they have won out of struggle."[59] He
understood that the Russians would not accept
assistance if it was conditioned upon the acceptance of
different views of faith and practice. The American
Disciples accepted these assessments. They continued
to send some financial aid for the Bible college and
general relief until the disruptions of 1929 closed the
school. In 1925, Russian churches in America which had
been affiliated with the Disciples withdrew to form an
independent Russo-Slavonic Union of Evangelical
Christians with John Johnson as president.[60]

    Prokhanov returned from his eighteen-month
stint in America for what was to be his last year in
Russia. He traveled triumphantly throughout his
country and observed firsthand the extent of the
penetration by the Evangelical Christians into the
various regions and among a growing circle of ethnic
Russians. His journey took him to the Ukraine, Siberia,

the Far East, and the Caucasus region. In Ukraine he visited churches in Kiev and Kharkov, the new capital. He journeyed to Siberia in August 1927 and visited the cities of Viatka, Perm, Tumen, Sverdlovsk (Ekaterinburg), Omsk, and Novosibirsk (the administrative center of Siberia). In the Far East, he reached the town of Ulala in the Altai Mountains, the capital of the Oisat Autonomous region. Here he selected the site for his ideal city, Evangel'sk ("City of the Gospel") and planted oak trees where the city would arise, at the confluence of the Bya and Catun rivers. In the Caucasus region he visited Piatigorsk, Kislovodsk, Armavir, and Kropotkin. In this area of multiple cultures, he found believers among the Ossets, Kabardinzi, Armenians, Georgians, and Gypsies. In central Russia, he reached Voronege. Wherever he went he found "newly formed district unions and councils; he experienced conferences, revivals, crowded meetings, repenting sinners, joyful faces." His experiences "strengthened [his] conviction that the spiritual awakening of Russia is spreading immensely."[61] Prokhanov had reported to Karl Borders in 1924 the size of the movement at that time: 1,500 registered congregations, 300,000 recorded baptized believers, and with families and adherents, a total group of one-and-a-half million.[62] In 1926, Burnham reported the movement was approaching two million strong. By the end of the decade and before the depredations of Stalin, that number had increased possibly twofold.

By 1928 Stalin had consolidated his power. Joseph Vissarionovitch Dzhugashvili, Stalin's given name, came from a little town near Tiflis, in the Georgian region of Prokhanov's origin. Stalin had attended a church school and been expelled from seminary, but not before he had been exposed to the poison of atheistic thinking. Having served as Secretary-General of the Central Committee of the Communist Party since 1922,

Stalin terminated the New Economic Policy (NEP) in 1928 and replaced it with the first of his Five-Year Plans. Stalin had stated in 1927, "The Party cannot be neutral in regard to religion." His Commissar of Education, Lunacharsky, said, "I should like in the most sadistic manner to root out and tear out this utter weed from our fields and gardens."[63] In 1929 the Bible school in St. Petersburg was closed, and the Evangelical publications were stopped. In April 1929 a new law affecting religion stopped preachers from traveling—effectively ending evangelism—closed women's groups, disbanded youth groups (other than the Communist Komsomol), and abolished the freedom of religious propaganda. Religious activity was limited to the performance of the "cult" within buildings designated for that purpose. In Leningrad, nine out of ten—in Moscow, three out of four—Evangelical churches were closed.[64] In August 1929, the continuous work week was installed, which gave no breaks for worship on Sunday. The Unions of the Evangelical Christians and the Baptists were officially dissolved.[65]

Prokhanov attended the World Baptist Alliance congress in Toronto in the summer of 1928. He was viewed by the Stalinist government as a conspirator in counter-revolution who accepted foreign aid as bribery from the international bourgeoisie. He was not permitted to return to Russia.[66] Prokhanov continued his work from a distance, traveling throughout Europe and America.[67] He wrote his autobiography in New York in 1933 and died in Berlin in 1935 at the age of sixty-six, from complications of diabetes.

The apostle Paul encouraged the early believers, "We must go through many hardships to enter the kingdom of God" (Acts 14:22). The fifty-year experience of the Russian evangelical awakening gives poignant expression to that reality. As difficult as those years were, they were only a prelude to the subsequent horrendous

treatment to be suffered by Russian believers under
Communist repressions for the next sixty years. The
Pashkov movement began as an attempt to revive the
spiritual life of the Russian people. Pashkov quickly
grasped the need for the biblical expression of faith and
for unity among believers. The resultant explosive
development within aristocratic society brought early
attention and quick repudiation by the state church.
Pashkov's removal in ten years left the movement weak
both in leadership and in its perception of how it should
develop as a church of Christ. Prokhanov's entry
brought vision, energy, and organization. He gathered
the scattered remnants of the Pashkovites and Stundists
and framed, almost single-handedly, the Evangelical
Christians as a closely knit, rapidly growing, confessing
body. Prokhanov enjoyed a forty-year time span for his
endeavor. His vision was of restoring apostolic
Christianity. His crucible was Russia with its shifting,
swirling mix of Orthodoxy, Imperialism, a nascent
peasant enlightenment, a burgeoning middle class, war,
revolution, civil war, constant repression, famine and
persistent poverty, a deeply-rooted religious tradition,
Western Protestant influences, and a militant atheism
buttressed by a looming Communist order. That
Prokhanov warped the movement into a shape that was
both an extension of himself and distinctly Russian may
perhaps be understood. The half-century achievement
was, nevertheless, a remarkable expression of faith and
insight into the essentials of Christianity. Subsequently,
the movement, decimated by Stalin's atrocities, moved
on into a denominational setting by its merger with the
Baptists in 1944. Yet the vision that drove the
Evangelicals of the Pashkov-Prokhanov era stands as a
beacon for modern Russia. Pure Christianity of the Spirit
and the Word of God is not to be centered in the
traditions of the East nor in the divisions of the West,
but in the truth from heaven. The Holy Bible, delivered

directly to the minds of the Russian people and
appropriated through their own efforts, can lead them
to be Christians only in a unified fellowship of believers.
With a faith settled on the foundation of the apostles,
they can practice the simple life described in the New
Testament, becoming the instruments of God for healing
their nation and leading Russian men and women into
the Kingdom of God.

Let Prokhanov's vision ring throughout Russia
as the third millennium dawns.

> It is firmly held by all believers in Christ, apart
> from any distinction of name or creed, that the
> church of the first century, the church of Christ
> and the Apostles, as it is revealed to us in the
> Acts and in the letters of the Apostles, is in its
> ideal aspect the model for the Church through
> all the future centuries, and will ever remain so....

> Only the restoration of a Church which had its
> origin in the spirit of primitive Christianity, with
> its all-embracing and creative religious power,
> will be able to overcome the spirit of unbelief as
> manifested in atheism, materialism, and free-
> thinking, and to prevent its further growth
> among the people of the world....

> Take the Old and yet eternally New Gospel as
> the foundation of your life, to rebuild it in accord
> with the teaching of Jesus Christ, and then the
> earth and the heaven will be new.[68]

---

[1] "During the two and a half years of war, Russia had
four prime ministers, three foreign ministers, three defense
ministers, and six ministers of the interior." John Channon, *The
Penguin Historical Atlas of Russia* (New York: Penguin Books, USA,
1995), 94.

[2] Ending over 300 years of Romanov rule.

³ St. Petersburg's wartime name.

⁴ The Petrograd Soviet of Workers' and Soldiers' Deputies. "Soviet" comes from the Russian *sov'et*, or "council," the supreme local body which elects deputies who serve in central congresses.

⁵ The government proclaimed amnesty for political prisoners, abolished discriminatory legislation, inaugurated the eight-hour day, restored the constitution of Finland, promised Polish independence, and arranged for the election of a constituent assembly. See Lionel Kochran, *The Making of Modern Russia* (Hammondsworth, Middlesex: Penguin Books, 1962), 245.

⁶ Germany supported Lenin's return from exile, for the Bolsheviks were considered a potentially destabilizing force that would further weaken Russia.

⁷ Reverses were experienced during this period. Lenin was forced to seek refuge in Finland from July through September, where he prepared his *State and Revolution.*

⁸ Trotsky's assessment, as presented in Kochran, 257. Estonia, Lithuania, and Russian Poland were given over to Germany and Austria; areas of Turkey were given up. The independence of Ukraine, Georgia, and Finland were accepted. Reparation of six million marks was agreed to. Russia lost one-third of its agricultural land and population, four-fifths of its coal mines, and half of its industrial base. By 1940 the Soviet Union would regain all territories lost in Brest-Litovsk.

⁹ e.g., Great Britain, through Arkangel'sk.

¹⁰ The *Cheka*, or secret police, had been formed in 1918 by Felix Dzerzhinsky. Concentration camps were established. Twelve thousand people were executed between 1918 and 1921. Channon, 97.

¹¹ Kochran, 265.

¹² Kochran, 269.

¹³ Ivan Prokhanov, *In the Cauldron of Russia*, 179-80.

¹⁴ Prokhanov, 181.

¹⁵ Prokhanov, 185.

¹⁶ Hans Brandenburg, *The Meek and the Mighty: The Emergence of the Evangelical Movement in Russia* (New York: Oxford University Press, 1977), 173.

¹⁷ Quoted by Brandenburg, *167.*

¹⁸ Prokhanov, 177.

¹⁹ Prokhanov, 174.

²⁰ The Baptist William Fetler played an important role among Russian prisoners of war when he was deported by the

government in 1915. In 1916 he organized the "Evangelistic Committee" for work among Russian prisoners in Europe. J. Mott, Methodist founder of the World Christian Student Union and pioneer of the ecumenical movement, was president of this committee.

[21] Petrograd was renamed Leningrad in 1924.

[22] Prokhanov in his autobiography, reports, "...we declared at one of our conferences the slogan: 'No politics, only the Gospel.'" Prokhanov, 172.

[23] Channon, 96.

[24] Prokhanov's words were recorded in the 1910 publication *The Baptist* #46, and cited in *History of the Evangelical Christian-Baptists of the USSR* (Moscow, 1989, translation by Lydia Loginova),159.

[25] The 1911 World Baptist Congress was the second such congress held.

[26] *History of Evangelical Christian-Baptists*, 193.

[27] That only fifteen delegates were present reflects the turmoil of the civil war years; it may also indicate some dissatisfaction with the union initiative.

[28] In fact, the two groups were not one in their views on major practices: both baptized adults, but the Evangelicals did not require baptism; both observed the Lord's Supper, but the Baptists practiced closed communion; both appointed elders, but the Evangelicals did not ordain clergy.

[29] It may be that "Prokhanov's rather erratic and enterprising nature was alien to the Baptist brethren, and they therefore preferred to remain independent" (Brandenburg, 134).

[30] Decimated by a decade and a half of persecution and under state pressure, the Evangelical Christians and the Baptists merged in 1944 to form the largest Protestant denomination in Russia.

[31] During the years 1921-23, the purge included the liquidation of 2,691 married priests, 1,962 monks, 3,447 nuns, and unknown numbers of laymen. (See Dimitry Pospielovsky, *The Russian Church under the Soviet Regime: 1916-1982*, 2 vols. (Crestwood, NY: St. Vladimir's Press, 1984), 31).

[32] Following the abdication of the Tsar and during the short life of the Provisional Government, the Orthodox Church moved quickly to remove the Holy Synod and restore the Patriarchate. On August 15, 1917, an All-Russia Council opened in Moscow and elected Tikhon (Belavin), Metropolitan of Moscow, as Patriarch of the Church, thus ending the imperial intrusion into

the affairs of the Church which had begun with Peter the Great. Prior to 1907, Tikhon had been the ruling bishop of the Russian Orthodox missionary archdiocese of North America. (See Pospielovsky, 31).

[33] Brandenburg, 174.

[34] Prokhanov, 212.

[35] Prokhanov, 213.

[36] Prokhanov, 213. Antonin died in 1926. Before his death he directed that the Peter and Paul temple in Moscow, in which he had conducted his services, be given to the Evangelical Christian congregation in that city. Subsequently, Prokhanov preached regularly in that building when in Moscow, and always to large audiences.

[37] Prokhanov, 213.

[38] Prokhanov, 216.

[39] The descriptions "golden age" and "golden decade" were used by Pollock (*The Faith of the Russian Evangelicals*, New York: McGraw-Hill Book Company, 1964, 80) and Sawatsky (*Soviet Evangelicals Since World War II*, Kitchener, Ontario: Herald Press, 1981, 28).

[40] Brandenburg, 166.

[41] Pollock, 76.

[42] Pollock, 77.

[43] Igor Troyanovsky, ed., *Religion in the Soviet Republics: A Guide to Christianity, Judaism, Islam, Buddhism, and Other Religions* (New York: Harper San Francisco, A Division of Harper Collins Publishers, 1991), 152.

[44] Brandenburg, 168.

[45] For a description of the Old Believers, see chapter four.

[46] Kalinin, named in honor of the president of the Soviet Republic at the time of this incident. The president took a personal interest in the arrest and the subsequent investigation.

[47] Brandenburg, 183.

[48] Brandenburg, 184.

[49] Brandenburg, 185.

[50] Vladimir Ilich Ulyanov (Lenin), seriously ill during the previous year, died on January 21, 1924.

[51] Prokhanov, 226.

[52] Prokhanov, 227.

[53] 5,000 New Testaments, 5,000 Bibles, 1,000 *Gusli*, 1,000 *Spiritual Songs*; see Brandenburg, 177.

[54] Printing continued from the last month of 1926 through to the fifth month of 1918, producing 35,000 Bibles, 25,000 New Testaments, 60,000 hymnals, 15,000 concordances, 40,000 "Gospel

Advisers" (a perpetual church calendar); Prokhanov, 228.

[55] Prokhanov, 229.

[56] Prokhanov, 228.

[57] Quoted by Brandenburg, 178.

[58] Karl Borders, "The Evangelical Church in Russia," *World Call*, May 1924, 14-17; Frederick W. Burnham, "What I Found in Russia," *World Call*, May 1926, 22-25, 34.

[59] Burnham, 25.

[60] A present-day assessment of the relationship between the Disciples and the Evangelicals is given by Albert W. Wardin Jr: "In spite of the enthusiasm of various leaders, the efforts of the Disciples in support of a Russian mission proved to be modest in investment and limited in duration.... Except for one or two keen observers, the leaders in this endeavor also convinced themselves that they were dealing with a movement which was restorationist, but from the evidence at the time and from later events this assumption proved to be false." See "The Disciples of Christ and Ties with Russia," *Discipliana* (Nashville, TN: The Disciples of Christ Historical Society, Fall 1992, Vol. 52, No. 3), 39.

[61] Prokhanov, 230-33.

[62] Borders, 17.

[63] Pollock, 81.

[64] Pollock, 82-83.

[65] Pospielovsky, 103.

[66] Pollock, 83.

[67] Including Bulgaria where, in 1935, he ordained Mitko Matheef, who subsequently established forty-two Evangelical churches in that country. Mr. Matheef presently resides in St. Catharines, Ontario where he was interviewed in preparation for this work.

[68] Excerpts taken from Prokhanov's "The Resurrection Call," a special letter of appeal he directed to the religious world just prior to his final departure from his beloved Russia in 1928 and recorded in the closing chapter of his autobiography, *In the Cauldron of Russia*, 263, 267, 270.

PART THREE

12

The Hunger

Fashioned by Winston Churchill, it was called the "Grand Alliance": a twenty-year pact between the Soviet Union, Britain, and the United States, signed in May of 1942 after Churchill had said, "Whatever is dangerous for Russia is dangerous for us."

The names of heroes and villains are well known to us and have become part of our permanent vocabulary: Hitler, Stalin, Roosevelt, Churchill, Khruschev, Brezhnev, Gorbachev, and Yeltsin. These were major players in World War II, the Siege of Leningrad, the arms race, the Cuban Missile Crisis, the Berlin Wall, and all of the Cold War and *Glasnost* which followed.

Whether a citizen of one of the superpowers or not, no one escaped the impact of these cataclysmic events. Generations to come will count their losses. Some lost precious peace of mind. For others it was billions of tax dollars. The Soviets saw Josef Stalin develop modern industrialization, but few of the benefits of this transition reached the masses since most of the gains were directed to the development of the nuclear arsenal and other military uses or to Sputnik I (1957) and other space ventures.

Stalin's leadership did, however, impact the masses—with deadly results. Early in his career as secretary-general of the Central Committee Stalin assassinated Leon Trotsky, his most powerful rival.

Seeing that the worldwide socialist revolution expected by Lenin was not to occur, Stalin moved swiftly to consolidate his power and organize a state economy. What is more significant for the present story is his determination to control every facet of Soviet life. During this early period alone, it is estimated that ten million peasants died. Historians continue to attempt to total the millions who vanished or were openly murdered in the years following.

Josef Stalin did not hesitate to target the Communist Party itself if he felt threatened by competing leadership. In the mid-1930s he unleashed a wave of intramural executions to bring his personal power to a peak. A deep hunger was left in the wake of Stalin's reign, a longing for freedom, for a better standard of living, and for safety from arbitrary arrest.

Nikita Khruschev's de-Stalinization did little to satisfy the legitimate hopes of Soviet citizens. Khruschev continued to bully and bluster against the West, a style of "diplomacy" long characteristic of Soviet Russia, the Red Army and Josef Stalin. Internally, he blundered badly in an attempt to improve agriculture, and his failure to provide freedom of conscience only prolonged the horror in the lives of believers.

Alexander Solzhenitsyn's *Gulag Archipelago* documented the dehumanizing treatment and unconscionable punishment of those who would dare to associate with someone who questioned "the State." In a smaller work, Solzhenitsyn cautions against confusing "Soviet government" with the people of Russia and succinctly summarizes the terrors of this century for the Russian people.

> In the first revolution (1917-1920), Lenin's curved dagger slashed the throat of Russia. Yet Russia survived. In the second revolution (1929-1931), Stalin's sledgehammer strove to pound Russia

to dust. Yet Russia survived. The third and final revolution [as Solzhenitsyn wrote in 1980] is irrevocably underway, with Brezhnev's bulldozers bent on scraping Russia from the face of the earth.[1]

Notwithstanding Solzhenitsyn's dire prediction, Russia survived, overcoming tremendous odds, but only because of the tremendous courage of the Russian people. One chapter that amply illustrates this bravery is the Siege of Leningrad,[2] another the killing fields of Magadan, still another the testing of atomic bombs within sight of the homes of the populace.

As horribly threatening as the slaughter and abuse of millions of innocents is, we now know there was a deeper, darker disregard of human dignity entrenched in the official Soviet mind-set. Human beings were robbed of their right to think and believe. As a Moscow taxi driver said recently, "Believe? Seems like a great idea, but I have been deprived of my ability to believe in anything." Or, as an intelligent forty-five-year-old St. Petersburg businessman observed, "I want my wife and daughter to be Christians. It is too late for me. My mind has been poisoned."

There are many stories which have come to light since KGB files have been opened. One of these is the story of Peter Vins, discovered by his son, Giorgi, who has now been allowed to read his father's file. Peter was arrested, along with many other pastors and church leaders, in 1930. Imprisoned for three years, he was released and shortly thereafter rearrested. Peter Vins died in prison and is buried at an unknown location. Like so many others, Peter Vins had counseled Christians to be faithful to the truths of the gospel.

The surprise is not in finding those who cry out in pain, "I cannot believe in God!" The surprise, considering the brutality of those seventy years, is in finding so many who boldly express such hunger for a spiritual message. Recently, echoing the sentiment of the millions now emerging from the dark night of Communist domination in the former Soviet Union, one wrote:

> Five years ago we could not dream of writing a letter abroad, but now everything has changed for the better. As to religion, we also witness great changes. In our city, they are going to build a huge church and a chapel in memory of the victims of Stalinism. Great changes take place in our souls as well. Now we, who lived in this atheistic country for so many years, witness great interest in religion among the people.[3]

Another, in a poignant letter, explores the "new" world of her society now and the promises of change.

> Lately, we are more often seeking spiritual and moral support in Christian philosophy. In our country, religion was laughed at as a result of powerful atheistic propaganda (by the way, very primitive propaganda), for seventy years. Thus people were deprived of moral and spiritual support. Communist ideals were substituted for Christian faith.

> [Communist] propaganda was also directed toward children in daycare and accompanied them all life long. The Soviet people could not buy Christian literature. There were no Christians schools where people could study the Bible. That is why there are few believers here.... It's a pity, but I am also an unbeliever; but I respect Christian philosophy very much and I believe that our world survived and did not fall to pieces for two thousand years only thanks to Christian

morality.[4]

As we spent time in Russia and in the other republics of the former Soviet Union, we met persons who would tearfully embrace a copy of the Scriptures. We met one who related the story of renting a Bible at the rate of one ruble per hour because buying one was too expensive. Grandmothers were met who lovingly, softly related their stories of faith, mingled with stories of family members who were led away, never to be seen again. Communities of believers of several hundred were encountered from whom nearly all the men "disappeared" while those left behind kept two or three Bibles carefully hidden from prying eyes.

Walking the streets of Russia today, visiting the cities and villages, observing the gatherings in the churches, and conversing with believers, one senses an exciting vitality. It is as though people are returning to life and breathing deeply of fresh air—in many cases the fresh air of the gospel. Even if some vote "Communism," even if many are struggling for daily necessities, the joy found in freedom of conscience and the freedom to hear the voice of God and to search for his answers are almost palpable. Surely, none could have been more thorough in the attempt to purge faith from the face of the Soviet world than the Communist leaders. But they failed! What they have done, in fact, was to sharpen an appetite for the satisfaction of spiritual need that is unparalleled in the twentieth century. We met people such as the gentleman who wrote:

> Our people need [the gospel], especially now in this dark and troubled period of history. They need support and faith; faith in Christ and his love for people; belief in something bright and beautiful, which makes us human beings. We are those who have been crushed, destroyed, burned

up, and scattered like ashes. The human soul resembles fertile soil. The seeds of kindness and love grow fast in it, and very, very soon they yield a rich harvest in the most worthless and meanest people....

Thank you for sowing such seed and calling for God.[5]

We recall a meeting with a young woman on the streets of a Russian city. Her darting eyes revealed that, as she now openly talked about Jesus and the gospel in this new day, she had fearful memories of the past. Indeed, she can look back on a home life with parents who were professionals...and believers. Now she was asking a question for anyone to hear: "Why didn't my parents share their faith with me? Sometimes I feel cheated." Then, she answers her own query: "If they had talked about Jesus, my siblings and I would have repeated it at school, and all of us would have been in danger." As it was, she reported it was often necessary for the family to move when local authorities became suspicious. As she related this story in the large lobby of a well known hotel, she would stop occasionally and nervously look around before continuing. "Not so long ago there would have been microphones in the potted plants," she explained, "and someone listening to everything I say."

It is not too much to say that this spiritual hunger for something more real than socialism, something more satisfying than Marxist-Leninist democracy, is a significant heritage of the Evangelical Christians who so valiantly proclaimed the Kingdom of God in their day. From the hearts of hundreds who died before firing squads, were imprisoned, were exiled to Siberia, or mercilessly ostracized for daring to speak the name of Jesus, there is left a promise—a promise of fulfillment to those who hunger and thirst for God. It is more than speculation to say that heirs of the Evangelical Christians carry on in today's Russia. While the embers of their faith live warmly in many hearts, the real people, the actual second and third generations of Evangelical Christians have been identified.

For example, Lubov Kuzdrezheva lives in St. Petersburg. She was a young child in that city during the siege—when it was still known as Leningrad. Her father had been driven away by the NKVD, the forerunner of the KGB, which later drove away her son as well. Her mother was killed by ruffians who broke into their flat looking for food during those desperate siege days. She was raised in a shelter, married a homeless boy, and they have made a good life together, working side by side in a steel mill. Lubov learned about Christ as a young woman and became simply a Christian. Having lived her life according to the principles of the gospel, she was thrilled when other Christians began visiting St. Petersburg after *Glasnost.*

Svetlana, the granddaughter of Ivan Stepanovich Prokhanov is in poor health, but in possession of many of the credentials of her famous grandfather, including some of his notes and hymn compositions. She spoke of his life and ministry. Many of the memories she preserves are of persecution, or the threat of it; and once the history is grasped, such memories are understandable.

These living souls are the children and grandchildren of those who knew similar yearnings to those clearly identifiable in the Russia of the 1880s, those who found spiritual sustenance in a simple, undenominational message. Whether the present fires of faith and hope in Russian hearts were directly ignited by those who lived at the turn of the century may be debated. Still, we must ask: Is anything that is truly of God ever silenced? Is hope ever so far from human consciousness that it does not continue to serve those who hunger for God?

Today, in the republics of the former Soviet Union, there is a hunger such as that of a young man whom we overheard, speaking at an Orthodox Church seminar in 1979. "We have experienced too much which prevents us from believing in Marx, either the old Marx or the young one, or in the scientific or the utopian one. At its best Communism challenges us to a unity of the body but without the soul—we want wholeness in its fullness."

---

[1] Alexander Solzhenitsyn, *The Mortal Danger* (New York: Harper Torchbooks, 1980), 3.

[2] Cf. Harrison Salsbury, *Nine Hundred Days* (New York: Harper and Row, 1969).

[3] Letter received by the authors, 1995.

[4] Letter received by the authors, 1992.

[5] Letter received by the authors, 1991.

I3
from the East?

L ike a drowning man grabbing for a straw, a
desperate country might grab and snatch for any
solution that offered the slightest hope. It may be unfair
to describe Russia as drowning, but the press now
describes the nation as sliding sickly into the third
world. Anyone with recent experience there knows
something of the daily distress for all except a small but
growing upper class.

The Russian infrastructure is ragged. Food
distribution is uneven, and the products on the shelves
are often of poor quality. Inflation is rampant. Medicines
and medical equipment are shockingly scarce, with
professional standards in medicine slipping in some
quarters. The political arena, from which some are
expecting deliverance, is undergoing a complete
demolition and rebuilding and so is likely to remain
confusing for some time. All of these potential, short-
term failures are sad, but the most urgent matter is that
"you cannot satisfy [the Russian soul] with material
things. People will soon realize it is not enough."[1]

Among the many symptoms of ill-nurtured
Russian souls is alcoholism. Reliable figures are hard to
come by. However, it is reported that alcohol
consumption in Russia quadrupled between 1940 and
1973.[2] To the extent that alcohol is used as an escape,
one may conclude that Marxism created a great desire
for flight during those years when it should have

blossomed, according to the promises of its progenitors. From a village on the shore of Lake Baikal in Siberia, one man wrote:

> Glasnost and Perestroika don't touch our lives here, and, judging by the government's reaction to recent events, these two concepts really have not touched the souls of our rulers. [We live in] squalor and dullness and physical poverty…. The only "prophet" we have in this village is a bottle of homemade vodka. "His excellency," the vodka, serves as a substitute for everything: for faith, hope, love of Christ, and justice.[3]

Russians have more than a millennium of relationship with Orthodoxy and several other forms of historic Christianity. The literature of early experiences testifies to these deep roots. Slashed, pounded, and scraped by the tools of Marxist socialism—in Solzhenitsyn's words—the Russian soul is even further from its nourishment than in pre-Revolutionary days. Are we to believe Russia's soul will find its nourishment and wholeness in the heritage of Orthodoxy simply because Orthodoxy is Russian? Is Russia's distress today the result of alien, Western influence dating from the determination of Peter the Great to have a "window on the West"? If the West would now simply withdraw from all major venues of Russian life, including areas of faith and ethics, would Russia be better off?

This debate rages within Russia and has done so since the sixteenth century. Many forms of nationalism now reassert themselves. Thoughtful persons who have learned to love the Russians cannot discard this question lightly. It is urgent to realize that Russians have a legitimate cultural stake in the way the Bible is interpreted and in the way the church is developed in Russian communities. While political and economic matters must be left to others, all would do well to heed Alexander Pushkin (1799-1837), one of the great poets of Russia. Pushkin, critical of historians who tried to adapt the latest system of the West for use in Russia, urged them to take into consideration the different conditions and special characteristics in the course of the historical development of Russia "whose history demands different things and a different formula."[4]

The Russian Orthodox Church is visibly alarmed by the numerous Western Churches which are "invading" the land. Does this mean that the Russian Orthodox Church holds the key to the spiritual vitality of the Russian people, simply because it is not Western? Is it the Russian Orthodox Church, as maintained through the Communist years, which in turn will bestow life, preserve hope, and give a brighter promise for the future? With all due respect for everyone involved, the answer is "No." The Russian Orthodox Church may not defend itself as the indigenous answer to the needs of the Russian soul. In the first place, we have already seen that the Russian Church was itself imported from Constantinople and the Byzantine Empire. For the first several hundred years of its life, the Church was ruled from Constantinople.

Some of this early history is as political and military as it is religious. As one example, consider how much Russian Church history is dated from A.D. 988 and the conversion experience of Prince Vladimir of Kiev. According to Preobrazhensky:

> While [Vladimir] was fighting against Byzantine rebel Bardas Phocas, a general who aspired to ascend to the imperial throne and had considerable forces at his disposal, Basil II appealed to Prince Vladimir, scattering generous promises in exchange for his aid. According to Hahja of Antioch, an Arab Christian historian of

the eleventh century, the treaty by which 6,000 Russian troops were sent to the emperor's aid stipulated that the 'Czar of Russians' Vladimir would marry Ana, sister of Emperor Basil, and that [Russia] would embrace Christianity....[5]

The historical reality is that the Russian Orthodox Church has never had a clear, well-defined position of independence from the Russian government—Tsarist or Soviet. If the Russian Church does not think for itself, is it possible that it might not readily counsel others to think for themselves?

There are other historic reasons why Russian Orthodox Church leaders, with their Eastern, Byzantine heritage, would do well not to appear too strident in their warnings about threats from the West. History testifies boldly that the Russian Church did not or could not respond appropriately to the changes that occurred in Russia during the nineteenth century. The Orthodox Church's response to the very serious distresses of the masses was equivocal. It was that equivocation which set the stage for the Evangelical Christian movement presented in this text.

The blurring of the lines between church and state has created the more serious problems for the Russian Orthodox Church. All too often the Church has become the propaganda wing of an ugly government.

Few pages in the history of the Church's subservience to the Soviet authorities can compare with the role the Orthodox Church played in the peace initiatives [following World War II]. At the first USSR Conference for Peace held in August 1949, Russian Orthodox Metropolitan Nikolai called the United States "the rabid fornicatress of resurrected Babylon...[who] is trying to seduce the people of the world while pushing them toward war."[6]

The utility of such virulent anti-American rhetoric for the Soviet government could hardly be underestimated.

It should be noted that there were members of the Church who resisted, even to death, any mindless link between Stalinism and the Orthodox Church. This individual bravery may be admired without supposing that it makes the Russian Church automatically innocent of collusion or that it is qualified to respond appropriately to the needs of the Russian people. The issue between the West and East is not as simple as determining who occupied the moral high ground in the geopolitical controversy at the end of World War II. The question is simpler: is the Russian Church capable of a well-qualified Russian, Eastern answer to the hunger in Russian hearts at the end of the twentieth century? History's answer is clearly negative. The Russian Orthodox Church's historic answer to the spiritual crises of her people has been to protect her structure and privilege rather than to provide nurture and healing. Like the wicked shepherds of Ezekiel 34, she has sustained herself to the detriment of her flock.

It is far too simple to say that the Russian Orthodox Church is better prepared to provide Russian answers because it is Russian. That Church has gradually become Russian, but it is and always will be an imported Church structure. Further, it is of little use to contend, as some do, that one cannot be Russian in any Church except the Russian Orthodox Church. This dictum would deprive believers of their freedom of conscience. One who seeks Christ must not be required by any hierarchy to follow a certain path or journey of faith but must be given the freedom to study the Scriptures and search for answers.

The Orthodox clergy's consternation about the coming of cults from East or West is admirable even though one might be forgiven for interpreting some of their expressed concerns as self-serving. It must be appreciated that the opening of Russia to outside voices has admitted dangerous groups who desire to control the minds of adherents. Orthodox priests have expressed sincere warnings which the Russian people should heed. However, they would do well to add, "It is about such cults that we give warning, while at the same time we grant that each one has the right to choose a course of faith."

On these matters, hear a Russian opinion, a very balanced one which is as optimistic as can be justified. Evgeny Barabanov, an art historian born in 1943, was denied emigration because he sent unpublished Soviet material out of the country. His essay "The Schism between the Church and the World" appears in a collection of six which explore Russia's future. He writes:

> Let us not hasten to accuse the Church. The fact that it has been forced to go "whither it will not" might still not have done great spiritual harm. The problem lies in *how* we define our attitude in this bondage, *how* we manage to accommodate both it and the triumphal paschal strength and joy. Currently some Christians bear this enforced bondage like a heavy obligation "for the sake of the preservation of the Church," while others have got used to it, acquired a taste for it, and have perhaps even come to like the contrast.

> But despite this manifest and indubitable submissiveness of the Church to the state, even the people who are far from being Christians are expecting some general renewal of it. They want to see the Russian Church an effective force that is capable of opposing mendacious ideological

bureaucratism with genuine spiritual values, of affirming moral principles and slaking the people's thirst with "the water of life."

People who know ecclesiastical life well are less optimistic. Having experienced within themselves all the terrible ailments and dilemmas of contemporary ecclesiastical reality, they are inclined to think that the Church will only be able to have an impact on society when society grows sufficiently free and democratic to liberate the Church from political fetters imposed by the state.[7]

Greek Orthodoxy has no special claim in Russia that justifies a dominant future. In a free land, on the basis of constitutional rights alone, Orthodoxy must be allowed her rights—and her rites. However, Orthodox exclusivism cannot be justified by history, as has been shown. Orthodox dominance is indefensible just because it is "Eastern" for the same reason other Eastern religions or philosophies must not be allowed to dominate. Elements of all of these are found in various sections of the former Soviet Union, including Islam and Buddhism. It will be interesting to see whether the Russian Church attempts to deal with all of these, as well as Catholics, Protestants, and evangelicals, in a manner which encourages a free conscience. Will this be the choice of the Russian Church, or will her choice be reactionary, returning to the times when other beliefs were controlled through her claim to a special link with government?

---

[1]   The words of a "thoughtful Muscovite, Alla Zismanova," who is quoted as she reflects on the poetry of Pushkin. See Mike Edwards, "Pushkin," *National Geographic* (Vol. 182, No. 3, Sept. 1992), 55.

[2] Basile Kerblay, *Modern Soviet Society* (Toronto: Random House, 1983), 290.

[3] Letter received by the authors, 1991.

[4] Quoted by Dimitry Blagov, from Pushkin, *Complete Works* (Moscow: USSR Academy of Sciences Press, 1937-1949, Vol. XI), 127; in *The Sacred Lyre* (Moscow: Raduga Publishers, 1979), 50.

[5] Alexander Preobrazhensky, ed., *The Russian Orthodox Church, 10th to 20th Century*, 2 vols. (Moscow: Progress Publishers, 1988), 1:5-7.

[6] Dimitry Pospielovsky, *The Russian Church Under the Soviet Regime: 1916-1982,* 2 vols. (Crestwood, NY: St. Vladimir's Press, 1984), 2:313.

[7] Evgeny Barabanov, "The Schism between the Church and the World," *From under the Rubble*, Alexander Solzhenitsyn, ed. (Boston: Bantam Books, 1974), 172.

14
from the west?

If the Russian Orthodox Church has been compromised by its relationship with Soviet government, Western evangelicals have often been used by the same government. If we must conclude Russia's answers will not be coming from the Orthodox Church because of its equivocal responses of the past, we must also sadly concede that Western evangelists have often been deceived by a complicated system they did not understand.

Both Catholics and Protestants—the latter more than the former—have gone into the former Soviet Union with noble intentions only to become instruments of a highly skilled propaganda enterprise. All serious students of this matter are indebted to Kent Hill of Keston College for a thorough study of the phenomenon.[1]

The situation was often like this: A Western evangelist, eager to speak about Jesus in the Soviet Union, would accept an invitation. Thrilled to be permitted into the country, he would travel paths laid out for him, listen principally to what he was told by government people and come home with pronouncements about "religious freedom" in the USSR. Soon Radio Moscow would quote the evangelist in its own defense.

Thus, in 1982 a Russian commentator in Moscow, Boris Bolitsky, responded to inquiries about religious freedom. He said he could produce all kinds of evidence on the subject, "but since this evidence from me and from Radio Moscow might seem suspect to you, for that very reason I will instead quote the testimony of unimpeachable witnesses." Bolitsky then quoted from a well known Western evangelist who had said, following his recent visit to Moscow, "I think there is a lot more freedom here than the impression that has been given in the States, because there are hundreds, even thousands of churches open. In Great Britain they have a state church, in other countries you have state churches, but here the church is not a state church, it's a free church."[2]

There have been Western extremists who have discredited all Russian churchmen as KGB agents, unable to tell the truth about anything. Others have been deceived in the opposite way, tending to believe anything they were told about open churches and freedom of conscience. And these blunders have been committed by most religious organizations. Parachurch ministries, according to Hill, have fared better.[3] The record of Western Christians throughout the Stalin and Khruschev eras has been so tarnished with clumsiness as to disqualify them to respond to Russian needs.

How well Western Christianity can identify with Russian people remains to be seen. All groups must not be tarred with the same brush, and there certainly have been outstanding examples amidst all of the short-term, paternalistic work. The worst of the latter may have resulted from residuals of the Cold War. After fifty years of lives lost and taxes paid, the West saw the Soviet system collapse. The temptation is to say, in effect, "The Soviet system was no good, and we must now show them how to run their country: free-market economy, democracy, Christianity, and all."

There is a great danger of arrogance in any mission which proceeds out of such thought patterns. Second, concepts of free-market economy and democracy must be held separate from efforts to proclaim Jesus. It is not true, as some have said, that "Christianity and capitalism go hand in hand." Christianity has never depended upon any one political system or economic plan but has spread and blessed people in all systems and all times.

Westerners must realize this: If Christianity is coupled with a particular political and economic structure, Westerners are committing the same error of which the Russian Orthodox Church has been accused— an improper relationship between church and state! Only when Westerners get beyond any feeling of superiority, beyond short-term evangelism in non-Russian languages, will they make some valid contribution to the deepest needs of the souls of Russia. Whether these contributions can be more than supportive of indigenous efforts remains to be seen.

Spread a good map of Russia before you, preferably one which notes the great variety of ethnic groups. Observe carefully the diversity of time zones and climates from the Bering Sea to the Black Sea, from Murmansk to Vladivostok. Consider the scores of ethnic groups, languages, and life-styles which dot the landscape. Ponder the European nature of cities in the west of Russia, where St. Petersburg is called "the Venice of the North," and contrast that with the Asian character of millions who live near the Sea of Japan or on the borders of Mongolia. Realize the enormous gulf of culture between the cosmopolitan citizens of Russia's major cities and the primitive lives of nomadic tribes and the village populations of Siberia.

Russia is a homeland for such incredible diversity. "Mother Russia" embraces many dissimilar children. Shall we call them "East" or "West"? What did Peter the Great's "Window on the West" mean to Irkutsk or Zhigansk? How does a "strong, central government" deal with such diversity and distance? What is the cultural "glue" which holds together this nation of many nations?

Mail from the corners of the former Soviet Union coupled with personal experiences in these far-flung regions makes it clear that the inner agonies of the souls of Russia are not confined to one region. It is not only the peasant who longs for meaning and reaches for hope, but it is also the scurrying resident of Moscow or Novosibirsk. When Russians ask, "What is the meaning of life? Why are we here? Is there more to life than this?", they may live anywhere, or they may belong to any ethnic or cultural group—they may be Eastern or Western.

It seems impossible that any human system of philosophy or faith will bring true satisfaction to the hunger of the souls of such disparate peoples. Personal experiences in Russia underline the dissatisfaction with Eastern ways among European Russians and vice versa. How these matters shall be worked out in government and education is the challenge of political scientists and academics. How these concerns are worked out for the nurture of the souls of Russia, whether East or West, is the true challenge to Christians.

Western church culture and structure are as out of place in some sections of Russia as they would be in central Africa or Tokyo. Just as Greek Church liturgy will not fulfill the needs of the Russian soul in such diversity, so Western church polity and homily will not meet the needs of all Russian people. As surely as the Russian Church has for centuries failed the peasants in far-flung villages, so the Western church has failed— and ignored—them for centuries.

The conclusion? Westerners do not have appropriate food for the Russian spiritual hunger as we approach the twenty-first century. The voice of God which must be heard by every seeking soul will not be clearly heard from sources that are either Eastern or Western in their essence.

Those from the West involved in mass evangelism—in Christian radio, for example—have faced the embarrassing question, "Why are you Western Christians so divided?" This is often followed by the observation, "You have had access to the Bible and the knowledge of Jesus Christ for all of these years we have been oppressed, and yet you are divided among yourselves." Westerners should not think it strange that Russians have decided that the West has not discovered the answers which the hungry souls of Russia seek.

Many Russians are avid readers of literature and history. They have felt deprived of fresh publications and good material during the dark years. When they do find a publication on the history of Christianity, they are often surprised to find the Russian Orthodox Church is completely omitted or treated but slightly, while Roman Catholicism and Protestantism are prominently included.

Westerners are known as exporters, and Western economies often thrive on exported goods. The young countries of the West, such as the United States, have also become exporters of ideas. Through the missionary enterprise, such countries have become exporters of Christianity. Remarkably the Christian faith, which centers in an Eastern crucifixion and resurrection, has been made to appear as a Western religion! Now these very believers are perceived by much of the world, including the former Soviet Union, as exporters of Christian faith; attempting to send back to the lands near its birthplace a faith which Westerners have reinvented as their own. They are perceived as exporting a faith which they have changed, rather than a faith which they have allowed to change them. It should not be concluded that this process has advanced to the point where the American missionary enterprise has become inadvisable. Yet we must consider that those in countries such as Russia will not always be eager to satisfy the hunger of their souls with the ministries of Westerners, however well intended.

Thoughtful Russians, as they emerge from limitations on what they can read about the rest of the world, are bound to wonder why the rest of us have not solved problems of racial confrontation, have not achieved some reasonable balance between conspicuous consumption and care for the homeless, have not chosen to invest more in cures for horrible illness and less in the military, have not found more interest in the development of great music and literature. As they ask these questions, each facile answer offered by Western Christians weakens their credibility.

Igor Shafarevich was born in 1917. He has served in the Soviet Academy of Science and is a former Laureate of the Lenin Prize. Through the Committee of Human Rights, he was an associate of A. D. Sakharov. Under the title, "Does Russia Have a Future?" Shafarevich writes:

> It has often been said that Russia cannot save herself alone and solve her own private problems.... It seems to me that the path to Russia's rebirth is the same as the path that will enable man to find a way out of his blind alley, to find salvation from the senseless race of industrial society, the cult of power and the darkness of unbelief.... The past half century has enriched us with experience that no other country has yet acquired. One of religion's most

ancient ideas is that in order to acquire supernatural power, one must visit another world, one must pass through death. That is how soothsayers and prophets are said to have arisen: "I lay as a corpse in the wilderness and the voice of God cried out to me...."

This is now Russia's position. She has passed through death and may hear the voice of God. But God makes history through men, and it is we, every one of us, who may hear his voice. Of course, we may not hear it. And remain as corpses in the wilderness that will cover the ruins of Russia.[4]

Russia's answer will come neither from the East nor from the West—but from above!

[1] Kent Hill, *The Soviet Union on the Brink* (Portland, OR: Multnomah, 1991).

[2] Hill, 170-171.

[3] Hill, 185.

[4] Igor Shafarevich, "Does Russia Have a Future?", *From under the Rubble*, Alexander Solzhenitsyn, ed. (Boston: Bantam Books, 1976), 294-295.

PART FOUR

15
from Above

Anye reported, "My friend scoffed when I suggested the kingdom of heaven is here. 'Where in Russia,' he protested, 'do you see any sign of the kingdom of heaven?'"

During several days in 1995, we had pored over those Scriptures with Anye that speak of God's great gift to the world through Jesus Christ, the inauguration of God's kingdom on earth, and its open-door policy for all the peoples of the world. When this understanding was shared, all Anye's friend could see was the all-too-clear evidence of misery, chaos, and evil. He did not understand that the reality of the kingdom's presence is to be inferred by the presence of God's grace rather than by man's progress. Personal regeneration, rather than national rejuvenation, leads the agenda of God's kingdom. When the people's hearts turn to God— when the rule of God is established within the lives of men and women—then will be borne out the truth that the "leaves of the tree of life...are for the healing of the nations" (Revelation 22:2). Jesus said, "The kingdom of God does not come visibly, nor will people say, 'Here it is,' or 'There it is,' because the kingdom of God is within you" (Luke 17:20b-21). The kingdom's presence in Russia is not disproved by the extent of the anguish people are experiencing, but rather is proved by the faithfulness of the many who remain constant in spite of the long years of suffering and deprivation.

The words of Jesus assure us, "Do not be afraid, little flock, for your Father has been pleased to give you the kingdom" (Luke 12:32). To his apostles he said, "I confer on you a kingdom, just as my Father conferred one on me" (Luke 22:29). And now, "This gospel of the kingdom will be preached in the whole world as a testimony to all nations, and then the end will come" (Matthew 24:14). Today, we can give thanks to the Father "who has qualified [us] to share in the inheritance of the saints in the kingdom of light. For he has rescued us from the dominion of darkness and brought us into the kingdom of the Son he loves, in whom we have redemption, the forgiveness of sins" (Colossians 1:12-13).

We contend that the kingdom of God is the first need of the Russian people, as it is the first need of any people. The good news of the kingdom and the concomitant practice of Christianity address both the spiritual and the physical needs of Russians. It should be clear that Colonel Vasili Pashkov and Ivan Prokhanov are not held up as perfect models of the kingdom of God. Many admirable elements of the kingdom were present, however, in the movements described in this book. It was these early leaders' declared intention to follow the teaching of the Scriptures. Even their harshest critics described them by saying, "Pashkovites recognize only the Holy Scriptures, rejecting the Holy Traditions."[1] That determination to be loyal to the teaching of the Holy Spirit in the Scriptures is upheld as the example that cries for emulation in our time.

Because the kingdom of God is universal, its essentials are appropriate for any culture. For people of good will who wish to grasp the possibilities of the kingdom of God, the following summary is offered.

1.   Newness of life results from the power of the living God at work in human life, producing a new creation. This is not an evolutionary, socializing process—the kingdom of God is not a utopian community in which humanity has progressed through science and sociology until they have discovered of their own experience how to rise above social ills. Newness of life equips human beings with the strength to cope with any system, whether one of freedom or one of oppression. As one comes into the kingdom of God, full privilege of citizenship is gained. There are no second-class citizens. The apostle Paul said, "You are all sons of God through faith in Christ Jesus, for all of you who were baptized into Christ have been clothed with Christ. There is neither Jew nor Greek, slave nor free, male nor female, for you are all one in Christ Jesus" (Galatians 3:26-28). While the new life is one of learning and growing, the citizen of the kingdom is received by God because of the death of Christ and is therefore gracious in receiving others (cf. Romans 15:1-7). Life in the kingdom is not gained at the culmination of human achievement as, for example, by graduation from a course of study. Rather, life in the kingdom begins with the "new birth" spoken of by Peter: "For you have been born again, not of perishable seed, but of imperishable, through the living and enduring word of God" (1 Peter 1:23). Citizenship in the kingdom of God is not only compatible with good citizenship in a modern state, but encourages good citizenship (cf. Romans 13:1-7).

2.   Life in the kingdom of God is a life of friendship and fellowship in which Christians bear each

other's burdens, worship and serve the God whom the kingdom honors, and become stronger because they recognize their need for God and each other. Dependence upon God and upon others in human relationship is a mark of character and strength. One who knows that others are needed to make life full and complete has come nearer to knowing himself. Dostoevsky's famous novel *The Brothers Karamazov* asks the question, "What is hell?" Dostoevsky's answer is, "[Hell] is the suffering of being unable to love." Love is relationship. The key to joyful, productive living is first, to be loved by God and to return God's love, then to be loved by other persons and to return their love. The picture of the early church in Jerusalem is one of sharing; of mutual helpfulness and fellowship: "All the believers were together and had everything in common. Selling their possessions and goods, they gave to anyone as he had need" (Acts 2:44). Pictured is a commonality evidenced by the spontaneous sharing of goods as the believers basked in the good fortune of having their sins forgiven through Christ.

3. The immortality of the human soul is fundamental to the kingdom. The good news of the kingdom recognizes the magnificent nature of humanity, neither limited to a finite world nor restricted by the achievements of a short life on earth. Hope, both as an essential ingredient of human joy, as well as in its fulfillment—more complete fulfillment than any political system can deliver—is the promise of kingdom life. Average life spans vary from culture to culture. For some it is enough to lengthen the life span through superior health care and improve the

quality of life as the years draw on. Kingdom life offers much more. Christians are not so otherworldly that they are unconcerned about this life. Human life in the kingdom of God is regarded as a time of preparation for eternal life, as well as a time when the good things of eternal life begin to be experienced. Significantly, experiencing the good life begins with serving others rather than being served. In Jesus' parable of the Good Samaritan (Luke 10:25-35) the professional religionists, the priest and the Levite, passed by the wounded man. Mere participation in formal religious practice is not religion of the heart, and these "respectable" persons are not portrayed by Jesus as living the abundant life. Rather, the gentle spirit which ministers to human distress while honoring God experiences the good life.

4. Forgiveness rooted in the sacrifice of Jesus, freely given to all who seek it by faith, lies at the heart of the kingdom life. One is made new in the kingdom when one acknowledges personal sinfulness, confesses inability to free oneself from sin, and turns to the salvation that Jesus offers through his death. Clothing oneself in Christ's righteousness, immersing oneself in the convicting Spirit of God, nourishing oneself by partaking of Christ, the "bread of heaven," are aspects of being "born of the water and of the Spirit" (John 3:5). This same new person in turn will be forgiving of others and this forgiving spirit among believers creates a congregation characterized by good will. We all offend and have been offended. Often gifts are offered as expressions of our longing to have the matter set right. All of us offend God by acting against his

holiness, goodness, and loving kindness. We go to God with gifts to express our longing to be reconciled to him. The original gift, however, is one God offers us: the gift of Jesus Christ. That is the meaning of Christ's death upon the cross. This loving gift is described in the Bible as "grace." "For Christ's love compels us, because we are convinced that one died for all..." (II Corinthians 5:14a). The second gift is the gift of ourselves to God. We are to "offer our bodies as living sacrifices, holy and pleasing to God..." (Romans 12:1). In the kingdom of God, it is impossible to remove our offenses from the sight of God by doing good deeds. When the offense is removed through trust in the death of Christ, however, life is then filled with good deeds, deeds of charity and worship offered in praise and gratitude for God's salvation in Christ (cf. Titus 2:11-14).

5. The Bible is the word of God, accurate in its original writing, fully translatable and frequently translated into the languages of the people. The Bible's message of redemption is presented by a merciful God for the understanding of all mankind and to be repeated by all who believe it. Parents conceive children through an act of love, and these children bear their images. Intelligent communication is possible between parent and child because of that shared image. There is tenderness and affection in the words of the parents when they guide, encourage, warn, and inspire their children. Similarly, God has created us as his children. In the beauty of his creation and in the kindness of his unconditional love for us, we recognize his goodness. He has sent his Son among us and provided us his word,

in the Bible, to warn, encourage, teach, and inspire us. The Bible is not accepted by Christians as God's revelation without careful study and research. Christians do not regard a copy of the Bible as a talisman or good luck charm. Nor are its printed words more sacred in one language than in another. It is the embedded message of redemption from a loving God that is sacred to citizens of the kingdom, the kingdom revealed in the Scriptures.

6. The church is the fellowship of those who have confessed Christ as the Son of God, who have been baptized into Christ, and thus have received both the forgiveness of sins and the gift of the Holy Spirit (cf. Acts 2:38). The fellowship of the church is the population of the kingdom of God on earth. This fellowship is faithful to the word of God as they learn it. It gathers in worship to honor the God who has given both forgiveness and promises. Filled with the Holy Spirit, the fellowship has life and grows in purity and spirituality. The church in every age looks to the Bible for the distinctives that mark God's dealings with his redeemed people and his will for the ordering of their lives and hearts. Various churches have arisen in many nations and in a variety of historical contexts. Some have been conceived in the political arena and diffused through military action. Others have resulted from efforts to correct abuses of religious structures which have drifted away from the declared intentions of Jesus Christ, who died to make his church possible. Can you imagine a portrait of Christ, over which have been placed thin layers of cloth? The cloth is so thin that a single layer leaves the original image almost

unaltered, but as one layer after another is added, the image grows dimmer and dimmer. The only way to see the portrait is to remove all the layers of cloth. Attempting to get a view of the church Jesus promised is something like this. One layer after another of history, philosophy, human greed, unmerciful judgments, and control have been laid over the original intention of Christ. Only when each person, studiously and in good conscience, returns to the first pictures of the church painted by the Holy Spirit in the word of God will one find the church as God intended it. The church of Jesus Christ is the contemporary manifestation among us of the spiritual kingdom of God. It is in the church that one finds the kingdom's citizens doing all things in the name of Jesus and living in expectation of his second coming, when they shall join the multitudes of all ages of the kingdom in eternal glory. Christ's purpose for his death and resurrection was that all his followers should unite in his apostles' teachings. Yet it is a sad fact of the history of religion that many believers have lost that dream of unity and replaced it with sectarian visions and narrow definitions of the faith. Today, Jesus calls us into oneness with him, with one another, and with God (cf. John 17:20-23). This good news is not a foreign message in Russia today any more than it was a hundred years ago. The kingdom of God is for all. As the "Gospel Christians" of the evangelical awakening in Russia discovered in the closing quarter of the nineteenth century and the opening quarter of this century, Russians can be "Christians only " by turning to the lordship of Jesus and following his teachings as preserved in the New Testament. Today, thousands are again becoming "Christians only," wearing no name but Christ's and accepting the responsibilities and privileges of life in the kingdom of God. Their citizenship in God's kingdom will also make them nobler citizens of Russia. Their answer and their hope is from above.

---

[1] A. Yartsev, *The Cult of Evangelical Christians* (Moscow: Atheist Publishing House, 4th Completely Reviewed Edition, 1930, tr. Yuri Dobrokotov), 4.

epilogue

The symbols are visible in Arkhangel'sk: city of Michael the archangel, situated on the 'divine' river beside the White Sea, bathed in twenty-four hours of sunlight for a few days in June. Yet the signs are not good for this city, which is almost five hundred years old, the city that momentarily attracted Peter the Great in his search for a gateway to the West. Electricity and central heat supplies are unavailable for long periods. A rusting fleet of nuclear submarines is docked just up the coast. Lenin's statue still dominates the central square. Cemeteries that contain the remains of soldiers and sailors of Western allies of the First and Second World Wars now also contain the bodies of young Russian men lost in the Afghanistan and Chechnya conflicts. Almost every street is named for a cathedral— streets that have for the most part been empty of churches for many years. A former Lutheran church was converted years ago to a concert hall and continues to serve that function. Evangelistic campaigns sponsored by Western interests periodically stir the city.

Yet even in this bleak landscape Yura, a Russian in his early thirties who walks with a cane to counter the effects of a bomb blast in Afghanistan, ministers to a young assembly of Russian believers intent on being Christians only. A small light shines in darkness—a good sign.

The parliamentary elections of December 1995 and the presidential elections of June and July 1996 indicate that democratic procedures are gradually taking hold. That the Communists were able to win one-quarter of the Duma's seats and garner one-third of the presidential votes reflect, no doubt, nostalgia for past security and a longing for former national and international glories. During the campaign it was disturbing to see the Orthodox Church courting nationalist elements in Russia, a Church formerly captive to one regime that used it as a means of control and humiliated by another that denigrated its God. A bill which would have reformed the landmark freedom of religion bill passed in 1990 was submitted to the Duma in the dying days of its mandate in early December 1995. Patriarch Alexei of Moscow was successful in bringing about the postponement of this bill which would have given reasonable equity to all religious groups. He is reportedly hopeful that the present Duma, even though Communist-dominated, will be nationalistic enough to accept a bill that will protect Orthodoxy's religious hegemony, both from external mission efforts and from domestic spiritual movements. Western evangelistic enterprises are concerned that the "open door" that has characterized the 1990s may be firmly closed.

The Russia of myth—the "superpower" of Communism, the "Gog" of evangelical dispensationalists, the "Mafia"-ridden crime haven of current sensationalist reporting—is not the real Russia. The real Russia is made up of people who yearn for a better day. They sense acutely the deprivation of moral and spiritual values which occurred during the long, black winter of materialistic atheism. Perhaps nowhere on earth is there a more deeply felt conviction that hope for the future is found in the truth from above. What is needed in Russia today is certainly not the revival of a nineteenth-century evangelical movement, nor the lionizing of yesterday's leaders, such as Pashkov and

Prokhanov. Indeed, as heaven presses in and draws us all toward our future with God, may the One who is the Way, the Truth, and the Life capture the hearts of the Russian people.

Bibliography

Works Cited:

Beasley, Charles Raymond and Forbes, Nevill. *Russia from Varangians to the Bolsheviks*. London: Clarendon Press, 1918.

Billington, James H. *Russia Transformed: Breakthrough to Hope: Moscow, August 1991*. New York: The Free Press, Macmillan Inc., 1992.

_____. *The Icon and the Axe: An Interpretive History of Russian Culture*. New York: Vintage Books, 1970.

Blagoy, Dimitry. *The Sacred Lyre*. Moscow: Raduga Publishers, 1979.

Borders, Karl. "The Evangelical Church in Russia," *World Call*, May 1924.

Brandenburg, Hans. *The Meek and the Mighty: The Emergence of the Evangelical Movement in Russia*. New York: Oxford University Press, 1977.

Broadbent, E. H. *The Pilgrim Church*. London: Pickering and Inglis Ltd. first edition, 1931; 4th ed., 1950.

Burnham, Frederick W. "What I Found in Russia," *World Call*, May 1926.

Channon, John. *The Penguin Historical Atlas of Russia*. New York: Penguin Books, USA, 1995.

Crankshaw, Edward. *The Shadow of the Winter Palace: The Drift to Revolution, 1825-1917*. London: MacMillan, 1976.

Dostoevsky, F. M. *Pis'ma v chetyrekh tomakh*. A. S. Dolinin, ed. Moscow, 1959.

Edwards, Mike. "Pushkin," *National Geographic* Vol. 182,

No. 3, Sept. 1992.

Heier, Edmund. *Religious Schism in the Russian Aristocracy, 1860-1900: Radstockism and Pashkovism.* The Hague: Marinus Nijhoff, 1970.

Hill, Kent R. *The Soviet Union on the Brink: An Inside Look at Christianity and Glasnost.* Portland, OR: Multnomah Press, 1991.

Jones, L. Wesley. *The Real Russians.* Huntsville, AL: Publishing Designs, Inc., 1995.

History of the Evangelical Christian-Baptists of the USSR. Moscow: Union of Evangelical Christian-Baptists, 1989.

Kerblay, Basile. *Modern Soviet Society.* Toronto: Random House, 1983.

Kochan, Lionel. *The Making of Modern Russia.* Hammondsworth, Middlesex, England: Penguin Books, 1962.

Langenskjold, Greta, and Baron Paul Nicolay. *Christian Statesmen and Student Leaders in Northern and Slavic Europe.* New York: George H. Doran Company, 1924; tr. Ruth Evelyn Wilder.

Latimer, Robert Sloan. *Dr. Baedeker in Russia and His Apostolic Work.* London: Morgan and Scott, 1907.

Lieven, Sophie. *Spiritual Revival in Russia.* Korntal, 1967.

Nichols, Gregory L. "Pashkovism: Nineteenth-Century Russian Piety." Master's thesis, Wheaton College Graduate School, 1991.

The Oxford Dictionary of Modern Quotations. Oxford: Oxford University Press, 1991.

Pollock, J. C. *The Faith of the Russian Evangelicals.* New York: McGraw-Hill Book Company, 1964.

Pospielovsky, Dimitry. *The Russian Church under the Soviet Regime, 1917-1982.* 2 Vols. New York: St. Vladimir's Seminary Press, 1984.

Preobrazhensky, Alexander, ed. *The Russian Orthodox Church, 10th to the 20th Centuries.* Moscow:

Progress Publishers, 1988.

Prokhanov, Ivan S. *In the Cauldron of Russia, 1869-1933*. New York: All-Russian Evangelical Christian Union, 1933; reprint, One Body Ministries, Joplin, MO, 1993.

Rothstein, Andrew, ed. *History of the Communist Party of the Soviet Union*. Moscow: Foreign Languages Publishing House, 1960.

Salsbury, Harrison. *Nine Hundred Days*. New York: Harper and Row, 1969.

Sawatsky, Walter. *Soviet Evangelicals since World War II*. Kitchener, Ontario: Herald Press, 1981.

Shagin, Boris and Albert Todd, eds. *Landmarks: A Collection of Essays on the Russian Intelligentsia*. New York: Karz Howard, 1977.

Solzhenitsyn, Alexander. *The Mortal Danger*. New York: Harper Torchbooks, 1980.

Solzhenitsyn, Alexander, ed. *From under the Rubble*. Boston: Bantam Books, 1974.

Troyanovsky, Igor, ed. *Religion in the Soviet Republics: A Guide to Christianity, Judaism, Islam, Buddhism, and Other Religions*. New York: Harper San Francisco, a division of Harper Collins Publishers, 1991.

Vesilind, Priit J. "Macedonia: Caught in the Middle," *National Geographic*. Washington: National Geographic Society, Vol. 189, No. 3, March 1996.

Wardin, Albert W. "The Disciples of Christ and Ties with Russia," *Discipliana*. Nashville, TN: The Disciples of Christ Historical Society, Vol. 52, No. 3, Fall 1992.

Yartsev, A. *The Cult of Evangelical Christians*. Moscow: Atheist Publishing House, 4th Completely Reviewed Edition, 1930; tr. Yuri Dobrokotov.

Works Consulted:

Alexeyev, S. *Russian History in Tales*. Moscow: Progress Publishers, 1975.

Alliluyeva, Svetlana. *Twenty Letters to a Friend*. New York: Harper & Row, trans. Priscilla Johnson Macmillan, 1967.

Bater, James H. *The Soviet Scene: A Geographical Prospective*. London: Edward Arnold, Division of Hodder & Stoughton, 1989.

Beeson, Trevor. *Discretion and Valour: Religious Conditions in Russia and Eastern Europe*. London: William Collin and Fontana, 1974, Fount Paperbacks, 1982.

Blumit, Oswald A., and Oswald J. Smith. *Sentenced to Siberia: Pastor A. Malof's Life Story*. Washington, D.C.: The Russian Bible Society, Inc., 1947.

Broadfoot, Barry. *Ordinary Russians*. Toronto: McClelland and Stewart, Inc., 1989.

Casey, Robert Pierce. *Religion in Russia*. New York: Harper Brothers, 1946.

Elliott, Mark R., ed. *Christianity and Marxism Worldwide: An Annotated Bibliography*. Wheaton, IL: Institute for the Study of Christianity and Marxism, 1988.

Fedotov, George P. *A Treasury of Russian Spirituality*. Vol. 2. Belmont, MA: Nordland Publishing Company, 1975.

Florovsky, Georges. *Ways of Russian Theology: Part One*. Vol. 5. trans. Robert L. Nichols. Belmont, MA: Nordland Publishing Company, 1979.

Grimstead, Patricia Kennedy. *Archives and Manuscript Repositories in the USSR: Moscow and Leningrad*. Princeton, NJ: Princeton University Press, 1972.

Kuroyedov, Vladimir. *Church and Religion in the USSR*. Moscow: Novosti Press Agency Publishing House, 1982.

Massie, Robert K. *Dreadnought: Britain, Germany, and the Coming of the Great War*. New York: Random House, 1991.

————. *Peter the Great: His Life and World*. New York: Random House, 1980, Wings Books Edition, 1991.

Moynahan, Brian. *Comrades: 1917—Russia in Revolution*. Boston: Little, Brown and Company, 1992.

Niebuhr, Reinhold. Introduction. *Karl Marx and Friedrich Engels on Religion*. New York: Schocken Books, 1964.

Radzinsky, Edward. *The Last Tsar: The Life and Death of Nicholas II*. Trans. Marian Schwartz. New York: Anchor Books, Doubleday, 1992.

Rutherford, Edward. *Russka: The Novel of Russia*. New York: Ivy Books, a division of Ballantine Books, 1991.

Schapiro, Leonard, ed. *The U.S.S.R. and the Future: An Analysis of the New Program of the CPSU*. New York: Frederick A. Praeger, Inc., 1963.

Shipler, David K. *Russia: Broken Idols, Solemn Dreams*. New York: Penguin Books, 1983.

Simon, Gerhard. *Church, State and Opposition in the U.S.S.R.* Trans. Kathleen Matchett. London: C. Hurst and Company, 1974.

Slate, C. Philip, and Stanley E. Granberg. *Reaching Russia: Evangelistic and Leadership Training Opportunities in the Former Soviet Union—Survey and Guidelines*. Abilene, TX: ACU Press, 1994.

Smith, Hedrick. *The New Russians*. New York: Random House, 1990.

Rothstein, Andrew, editor. *History of the Communist Party of the Soviet Union*. Moscow: Foreign Languages Publishing House, 1960.

Taubman, William, and Jane Taubman. *Moscow Spring*. New York: Summit Books, 1989.

Ware, Timothy. *The Orthodox Church*. Hammondsworth, Middlesex, England: Penguin Books, 1963.

Walters, Philip, ed. *World Christianity: Eastern Europe*. Eastbourne, E. Sussex, England: Keston Book No. 29, MARC International, 1988.

Wurmbrand, Richard. *Tortured for Christ*. Glendale, CA: Diane Books, 1967.